A Newcastle Lass

Irene Richardson

Copyright © Irene Richardson 2025

All Rights Reserved

No part of this book may be reproduced or transmitted in any form or by any means, electronic or mechanical, including photocopying, recording, or by any information storage and retrieval system without the written permission of the author, except where permitted by law.

Contents

Acknowledgment ii
About the Author iii
Prologue 1
Chapter One Grace 6
Chapter Two Aunt Mary 9
Chapter Three Henry 13
Chapter Four Avondale Road 21
Chapter Five Charlie 26
Chapter Six Christmas 30
Chapter Seven Confessions 36
Chapter Eight Unwanted Strangers 41
Chapter Nine Harry 48
Chapter Ten New Beginnings 52
Chapter Eleven Mother and Toddler Group 58
ChapterTwelve Isabella 63
Chapter Thirteen Tommy 68
Chapter Fourteen Lord and Lady Park 75
Chapter Fifteen Parker Street 82
Chapter Sixteen Tommy's Plan 88
Chapter Seventeen Moving House 96
Chapter Eighteen Tynemouth Sands 104
Chapter Nineteen Productivity 108
Chapter Twenty Contentment 112
Chapter Twenty-One Family Outings 117
Chapter Twenty-Two Millie 123
Chapter Twenty-Three Mystery Trip 126
Chapter Twenty-Four Blackpool calling 130
Chapter Twenty-Five Joan's Story 141
Chapter Twenty-Six Jonny 146

Chapter Twenty-Seven Uncle Jim...150
Chapter Twenty-Eight Love at last 157
Chapter Twenty-Nine Mary Ellen...160
Chapter Thirty Albert 164
Chapter Thirty-One Albert...169
Chapter Thirty-Two The Date Factory..176
Chapter Thirty-Three The Bus Trip 180
Chapter Thirty-Three War ended 183
Chapter Thirty-Four Alec..188
Chapter Thirty-Five In the money 193
Author's Note..200

This book is dedicated to my grandmother, Isabella.

Acknowledgment

Thanks to my wonderful husband who has been my support and my rock during the writing of this book.

About the Author

Born in Byker, a district in Newcastle upon Tyne where the book is set. Irene lived in Newcastle for 21 years and then moved to Scotland in 1967, newly married with her husband. Still living in Scotland today but even after all these years, never forgets her "Geordie Roots."

Covering three generations of family, this compelling down to earth story tells of the poverty, hardships, abuse, survival, and determination of Newcastle Lasses.

This is her first novel and hopefully more to come.

A Newcastle Lass

Prologue

Growing up in the Byker area where everyone was poor—we did not know it then—but so was everyone else in the same situation.

Streets upon streets of two-bedroomed old Victorian terraced houses, all looking the same. Brick houses, grey with age. Net curtains at the windows.

The only heating was from a coal fire, The Coal shed being in the backyard. There was no hot water, just a cold water tap in the scullery (kitchen).

There was no bathroom, and the toilet was housed in the backyard. In winter, the pipes would freeze, so a candle was lit to prevent them from freezing. Toilet paper consisted of squares of Newspaper hanging on a nail hammered in the wall.

You did not stay long in there, it was the domain of giant, hairy spiders whose main aim was to fall on your head and get tangled in your hair.

Bath time for families was usually a Friday night. The tin bath hung on the inside of the coal shed in the backyard.

The bath was set in front of the coal fire in the living room. It was filled with pots of hot water heated on the gas stove. When the water got cold, it was topped up with freshly boiled water. After awhile, the water turned yellow when the bairns did a wee in it. Hard luck if you were in there last!

Winters were harsh, the inside of the bedroom windows were often frosted with ice and Dad's Army Topcoat would come in useful as an extra blanket.

Meals were simple and repetitive. Everything was either fried in the frying pan, chips cooked in beef dripping in the chip pan (the most used pan in the house) or a stew made from cheap cuts of meat with Suet dumplings or a slice of bread to make the meal go further. Sometimes made into pies with pastry lids. Chicken was for Christmas, a lovely, rare treat.

Neighbours would not see any other family go hungry. Families were there for each other and were large with several hungry mouths to feed. Often a knock at their door and a neighbour standing there with a pot of soup or broth for the bairns, a few freshly baked scones. Sometimes it would be clothing that their siblings had grown out of and were still wearable, families would always be grateful for anything, especially hand-me-downs. Everyone shared what little they had.

Men worked in the engineering factories, coal mines, shipyards, and dockyards. Some were skilled, others were semi-skilled, and the rest were labourers. An extremely hard life with low wages, and poverty in most every home in Byker.

Front doors were left open, as there was little of value to steal. Life in Byker was tough, with hardship woven into the fabric of every home.

A Newcastle Lass

Start of the demolition of the streets of Byker.
photograph courtesy of Ian Krause

The Byker Wall where families were housed after demolition of Old Byker.
Some were housed in other areas where housing was available splitting up the community and the close bond of friends and families
photo courtesy of Trevor Ermel

Irene Richardson

*Map showing the streets of old
Byker before demolition.*

Once old houses and streets were demolished, the Byker Wall was built. A winding wall of flats which were designed to mask the noise from the planned motorway to be built.

Some called it an innotive piece of modern architecture, others called it a monstrosity.

The motorway was never built! The Byker Wall is still standing today, a permanent reminder of a plan that never came to fruition.

A Newcastle Lass

And so the Story of a Newcastle Lass begins …..

Grace and Isabella Mary

Photograph by kind permission/ courtesy of Emma Dixon

Irene Richardson

Chapter One
Grace

From the moment Isabella was born, her mother, Grace knew that the baby she had just delivered was the most precious thing in her life. A beautiful and innocent baby girl, whom she adored and loved from the minute she came into this world. Grace decided to name her Isabella, after her grandmother and Mary, after her aunt.

Grace made a promise to Isabella, that she would not have to suffer the kind of life, she, Grace had now. Why, oh why, had she not seen through Henry earlier! He was a cheat and a liar. He knew exactly how to get any woman, with that handsome face and cheeky smile, which he used to get what he wanted. How did she fall for that! He might change his ways now that he has become a dad. Grace had her doubts!

Grace's life with her husband Henry, was not a happy one, to say the least. Over the years of their marriage, Grace endured both mental and physical abuse at his hands. She never knew what mood he was in. One minute he was loving and smiling. The next he was an evil bastard with no thought of the mental and physical abuse he was inflicting, and no regrets either. Over the time Grace had been with him, she realized that Henry was willing to do whatever it took to keep her in line.

Henry did not know the meaning of compromise. Apologies were not in his nature. He was 100% right all the time. And whoa betide if Grace answered back.

It had started early on in their marriage by criticizing tiny things she said or did, she felt she could do no right in his eyes. Then she withstood the worst of his outbursts of temper, Grace was never sure of what mood he would be in when he walked through the door. She was on tenterhooks most of the time.

The physical abuse started with the odd slap across her cheek if she had answered back. It gradually escalated into a beating, for what reason or why, she was at a loss. Grace began to believe what Henry had said that she was not being a good wife. She promised she would try harder to please him.

Henry liked the ladies and was not one to be tied down with responsibilities and was wishing he were somewhere else now. His immediate reaction was to flee, instead of facing up to things.

Henry was seeing a barmaid called Elsie on the side. It was a win-win situation, Cheap beer, a warm bed, and someone who seemed eager to please. Elsie was a more than willing partner. What Henry did not know was that Elsie had other men too who paid for "willingness." Surely, he should have known this as she would ask him for money afterwards. Henry thought she must be short of cash. Elsie never charged him the full rate, claiming she had a soft spot for him, and Henry, blinded by his own desires and needs, never questioned it.

He thought he was God's gift to women, and they could not resist his flattery. He had had his fair share of them and bragged about all the women he had bedded to his mates. Unbeknownst to Henry, they were getting a bit fed up with his bragging and all the details. In fact, they called him, "Mr. Bighead with a little Plonker."

Henry was not what you would call handsome, he had a cheeky chap look with a beautiful smile that described him best. He knew all the right things to say to a woman, how to flatter them and make them laugh. If they enjoyed his flattery, then he was in with a chance. Henry enjoyed the game of chasing and bedding them and knew that he was not the type to be with just one woman. He liked to play the field. Plenty of time to settle down yet.

Henry was now married; his new wife was having a baby and everything else that came with it. "Bloody Hell, how did all that happen? What a damned nightmare!

Grace thought back to the day she met Henry for the first time. It was at her Aunt Mary's house in Byker.

Chapter Two
Aunt Mary

These days, Aunt Mary did not keep too well and was becoming quite frail with age. She did not go out and relied upon her neighbours to help with her shopping etc. They were kind and did not mind running errands for her. They used to say, "No bother, Mary I was going to the shops anyway."

"You know, I could be ill one day and would hope some of my neighbours would help. What goes around, comes around," I say.

Now in her late sixties, Grace's health had taken a heavy toll on her body. Her constant ailing health meant her joints and muscles ached all the time and it was such an effort to do the simplest of tasks and due to her illness, she looked more like a woman in her eighties. It felt like her body was betraying her, with each ache and pain a reflection of a life filled with struggle.

Mary looked forward to her Niece Grace's visits. Grace took the train from North Shields every month to Heaton Station and walked from there to her aunt's house on Avondale Road. She loved these visits. Aunt Mary had a wicked sense of humour, and they laughed all the time she was there. Grace was still smiling hours later when she boarded the train to go home to North Shields.

The following month, Grace was due to visit Mary today, and so Mary asked one of her neighbours, Nellie to buy a mixed choice of cakes from the bakers and a pint of milk for her coming. Mary told Nellie to buy an extra six Cream cakes for herself, her husband Tommy and their four bairns as a treat. "Oh Mary, you are so kind, thank you, I've not had a cream cake for years; we just can't afford them."

Grace arrived about 11 o'clock. Mary's heart was full of love for her niece and when she arrived it was as though the Sun had come out. She had such a beautiful face and Mary gave her a kiss and a big hug.

"Come on in Grace, I have just put the kettle on. One of my neighbours went to the bakers and brought me back some lovely cream cakes. Hope you are hungry."

Mary and Grace were having their cup of tea and cake when suddenly there was a loud knock on the door. Aunt Mary asks Grace to see who is at the door.probably neighbour going to the shops.

When Grace answered, Henry's gaze fixed on her. He had never seen such a beautiful girl, with porcelain skin, long dark hair, and perfect rosebud lips he wanted to kiss.

Grace broke the silence. "Can I help you?" Henry was mesmerised.

"I've come to see Mary," Henry replied.

Mary heard from the kitchen, "Come on in, Henry."

Mary was sitting in her usual comfortable chair by the fire where she always was. Her legs were now "tartan legs" which in Newcastle means legs that have been burned by sitting near the hot fire for years.

"How are you, Henry?"

"Yes, I am okay, thanks Mary, just off to the Betting Shop to put some money on a horse. It was a hot tip from a fella in the pub who knows a thing or two about the gee-gees. Are you wanting a flutter today?"

"Got a fancy a for a horse running in the 3.30, called Geordie Lad, saw it in this morning's paper, put a tanner each way on me for me please," Mary replied.

Grace saw Henry to the door. He wanted to see Grace again and blurted out, "Do you fancy going dancing on Saturday with me?" Grace was surprised, she did like dancing, so yes, she would. Henry planned to meet her outside the dance hall on Saturday at seven.

Henry's horse won 25/1 that day. Marys did not.

He collected his winnings with a feeling of triumph, heading straight to Parrish's store, and bought himself a new white shirt for his upcoming date with Grace. 'Got to make an impression,' he thought. Parishes was a local department store with several floors.

Irene Richardson

You could buy everything from clothes to housewares, furniture to jewellery, carpets, crockery, shoes and everything else.

In those days when folk were poor, everyone got a Provident Ticket for a certain amount. You would make weekly payments to the Provident Man, or "Provy Man" as he was known, until the ticket was paid off. Once it had been paid in full, another one was provided if wanted for the next purchase. This was the most common way to buy goods. Parrish was one of the several stores in Newcastle that accepted Provident Cheques or known as Provy Tickets

Chapter Three

Henry

Saturday came, and Henry met Grace outside the Ballroom in Newcastle City Centre as arranged. He paid the entrance fee of one shilling. He had money left over from his horse winnings to buy a couple of drinks for them too. Even enough to buy them a bag of chips afterwards.

They walked to the train station eating their hot chips with salt and vinegar on them. Mary had to get the last train back to North Shields. Henry held her hand and said all the right things, everything a young girl wanted to hear. So, when Henry bent to kiss her, she did not refuse. The train arrived and they said goodbye but had arranged a date for the following Saturday.

The friendship blossomed very quickly, and Grace was starting to fall for Henry. After a short while, Henry's advances became more serious. Despite her reservations, Henry convinced her that this was a natural step for couples who cared about each other. He ended up raping her, telling her all the girls let their boyfriends do this when they loved each other. She felt ashamed but did love him in her own naïve way. She thought if this was the way to keep him happy and please him, then she would let him have his way because they loved each other, didn't they?

Grace did not enjoy the experience, and he hurt her, but it did not seem to bother him, he did not even ask her if she was okay. Grace got on the train quite traumatized and cried all the way home.

'It would just be the once,' she thought. Her mother had never told her the facts of life, and this part was a real shock to her, but she soon learned that Henry wanted to do this every time they met over the next few months.

Henry enjoyed the chase and bedding a woman and would put it down to yet another notch on his belt.

He soon became a bit bored; he did not feel any excitement with Grace. She just shut her eyes and lay there! He was going to break up with her as he was courting another young girl from Clydesdale Road who was a bit more experienced.

The next time he met Grace; he had already made up his mind—he was going to end things. But when he saw her, she was in an awful state, crying and sobbing uncontrollably, tears rolling down her cheeks and her nose was running.

"Bloody hell. What is it? What is the matter?" Henry asked her between sobs.

Grace said, "I'm having your baby, and my Dad wants to see you."

A Newcastle Lass

On hearing this he was furious and shouted at Grace, "Why did you let this happen? Did you not do as I told you after we had been together?" He was enraged and of course Grace believed it was all her fault. How could she be so stupid. Henry arranged to see her dad on Sunday to sort things out.

Grace met Henry as he got off the train at North Shields station on Sunday to see the family as arranged. Her house was close to the railway station, about a ten-minute walk. Grace had thought he would have kissed her but no nothing. He just walked on.

The family home was a grand Victorian stone house in a well-to-do area of North Shields. It had a garden in the back, a garage and drive at the front for her Dad's car. Henry was impressed and thought that Grace would eventually inherit all this. What a result!

Grace led them to the front room, where her parents, James, and Nora Bolam, were sitting on floral velvet armchairs. Henry glanced around; everything looked classy and expensive. He would go along with what her Dad suggested. Let us hear what he has to say.

"Now then young man," started James, "I do believe you have not been treating our daughter Grace with the respect the way she deserves. You have gotten her pregnant, not what we would have expected at her age, so what do you have to say for yourself?"

Henry did not expect this and was a bit tongue-tied for a minute. He gathered his thoughts and said, "Well I love Grace, and she loves me, so we should get married now and quickly rather than next year.

I was planning to ask her to get engaged soon and to be married next year. I have been saving for an engagement ring but had to pay off the overdue money for my Mam and Dad's rent arrears."

This sounded convincing to him. He felt quite pleased with this quick thinking and wondered if they would fall for it.

James listened to Henry and thought that he was lying through his teeth. 'Did he think he was going to swallow this line? He thinks I am a stupid old man. Well, Henry, you just wait and see.'

"Right then lad let us get down to it. No time to waste." After discussions with Dad and Mam, it was agreed that they should be married very soon.

The wedding had been arranged by Grace's parents, who spared no expense in planning the event. Invitations were sent to their friends and relatives for the wedding reception which was held in a hotel in North Shields with no expense spared. Grace was slender and the baby was not showing, so no one knew otherwise.

During the courtship Grace had thought Henry had been a courteous person and caring boyfriend. But little did she know whom she was marrying?

The wedding day was perfect, and Grace knew she had made the right decision when walking down the aisle on her dad's arm and saw Henry waiting at the bottom of the aisle, the love of her life.

Henry on the other hand, looked around at the number of guests attending and thought, 'how much is this costing? A few pounds for sure these folks must have a lot of money.'

The wedding ceremony passed in the blink of an eye. Grace was in a dream; she was marrying the man she loved she was not aware of seeing his worried face. He was feeling tied down and caged. The short ceremony was over in a flash and the next thing they were walking back down the aisle. He did look smart and handsome. Her parents, however, did not approve of him. Their daughter deserved better, but Henry would have to take responsibility seriously now and make a home for their daughter and the baby.

Grace's dad helped get a rented one-bedroom house as a start for them and as a wedding present they paid one year's rent to get them started. By then Henry would have saved for the future to better themselves.

It was quite to come down for Grace when she saw the house, she was to start her married life bringing up a baby here. The truth of the matter was that her parents had spoiled her growing up and she was not fully prepared. But this would be a start for them, and she was having Henry's baby, they would be a family.

With her parents having paid the rent, Henry could afford to go into Newcastle to see his mates and buy a couple of pints of beer. He could also afford to buy the odd pack of cigarettes. He usually smoked Woodbines as they were the cheapest, but nowadays, splashed out on a more expensive brand.

Grace stayed at home where she belonged, not knowing what Henry was up to and blissfully unaware at what he did. She was content keeping her home clean and tidy, cooking and baking as a good wife should do.

Henry felt trapped. He was not ready for marriage or children, not like this. These days, Grace was always whimpering, moaning, and crying. He was obliviously unaware of the fact that her hormones were all over the place, oh how did you ever get tied up with this one?

The baby was due in three months' time, and he did not have any paternal feelings at all, plus the fact that he did not love Grace and in his eyes, this had ruined his life. He felt completely hedged in, he did not want a baby and wife, this was ruining his life, he felt really sorry for himself.

Henry was at the counter of his local pub ordering another drink. A girl who had been eyeing him up for ages, came up to him and began to chat. They had a couple of drinks together. She was nothing to look at, but she was eager enough to slip out into the back lane, behind the pub with him. Cannot be fussy, getting it offered for free, he thought. So off they went out through the back door of the pub.

Just then his mate, Arthur shouted to him "Henry, get your ass over here. Your Mrs. is in trouble. Think she is having the baby."

By the time Henry got home it was all over. Grace had given birth to a tiny boy—just six months along. The baby had not survived. Grace looked at his tiny face and welled up with emotion. He only weighed four pounds; she secretly called him James after her dad.

When Henry arrived, he took one look at his baby who was lying, covered up on the bed.

"Can't you do anything right woman; you cannot even have a healthy baby! You are pathetic. I cannot deal with this now!" and with that, he stormed out of the room, knocking the midwife sideways in his path. Grace was mortified and was in total shock. The midwife sorted everything and cleared up.

"You get some sleep pet; I'll be back in the morning."

Grace was distraught, what kind of man had she married? She was exhausted and started to drift off to sleep. As she did, a poem she had read some time ago resurfaced in her mind, vivid and clear, as if it had never left.

God, why did you take my precious baby?
I know he was tiny and not ready
For this world, but if only for a short while
He would open his eyes and give me a smile
To hold him close and feel his soft breath
Instead of joy, I am faced with his death

Irene Richardson

God, in your wisdom. It was not to be

He is now your little angel, look after him for me

Grace fell into a deep, exhausted, and troubled sleep.

Chapter Four
Avondale Road

All her life, Mary had lived in the same house on Avondale Road. She was born and grew up there.

When she left school, she went to work as a Secretary at Atkinson and Sons who were local Coal Merchants. She did enjoy her job. Mr, Atkinson, the owner had three sons, the two older ones, Freddie and Billy delivered the sacks of coal to all the houses in Byker and the surrounding areas. Mr. Atkinson drove the lorry, he was in his 50s now and did not do any heavy lifting, left that to his burley sons.

The youngest son Alan was of slim build and had a weak chest, so he worked in the office alongside Mary. They got on well. They had the same sense of humour and interests in common.

When Mary was 25 years old, she lost both her parents in a fatal accident. They were crossing busy Shields Road, deep in conversation and not paying attention and a tram ran into them. Her father was killed instantly, while her mother suffered severe injuries and was rushed to the hospital. She was in a coma due to an injury to her head. Mary sat by her bedside for five days before her Mam passed away peacefully in her sleeping state.

Mary was devastated and inconsolable. She threw herself into her work as she did not have many friends her age who were not married with babies and toddlers in tow, so she did not have much of a social life either and as such, spent her free time reading or going for walks.

Mary was an only child and was left the house, its contents, and a generous sum of money in a savings account at the bank, which she did not know about. Her parents had opened a savings account when Mary was born for her future, it was quite a considerable amount. Mary was smart, just like her parents, she did not need much money to survive and managed to run the house costs, food, and other essentials on her wages and put any extra money into the bank account.

One day in Winter, she slipped on black ice on the pavement as she was walking to work, which resulted in a fractured hip, a broken arm, and a cracked rib.

She obviously needed to give up her job. Thank goodness she had her savings.

Neighbours used to call and ask if she needed shopping, for which she was incredibly grateful for. When anyone had been to the butcher's shop, they said that Charlie the owner was asking after her. Mary used to shop there for her parents when they were alive and got on well with Charlie, they had the same sense of humor and shared interests.

When she got home, she found he had put in an extra sausage or two and a couple of extra slices of bacon in her shopping bag. "What a kind man," she thought. Mary gave these extras to her next-door neighbor, Aggie, who had 4 bairns to feed.

Charlie the butcher, had lost his wife Margaret several years ago, what a gentle, kind woman she was. Margaret died in Childbirth along with their baby boy. Charlie lived a quiet, but lonely life since she passed away. He went to the local pub a couple of nights a week to have a few pints with some of the regulars. It was a way to get out of the house and meet like-minded friends to chat away the evenings over a couple of beers. A game of darts, dominoes, or playing cards. Charlie was good at darts and always won.

Mary, once she was walking again, did her own shopping locally and went to Charlie's Butcher shop. He was pleased to see her. They did like each other, and they both knew that there was some kind of attraction between them. Charlie plucked up the courage to ask Mary out and she said Yes, she would love to go out with him. He took her for lunch in Newcastle to a lovely small but cosy restaurant on the quayside. This restaurant specialised in fresh fish. They had the Catch of the Day which was Dover Sole cooked in a lemon parsley butter sauce and accompanied by new potatoes and peas. It was delicious and although they were quite full, they could not resist an ice cream to finish. Mary chose Stawberry and Charlie had the Chocolate.

They set off back home feeling very full. Mary asked Charlie in for a cup of tea. He said, "Oh Grace, I would love to, we have done so much talking my throat is dry."

Charlie gave her a little kiss when he left to go home. He wanted to give her a big kiss and more but did not want to push her away. He would know when the time was right.

They saw each other regularly and went for outings to the coast in Charlie's car. They ventured further into Northumberland to see the many coastal towns and villages.

Northumberland was a beautiful county, and there were plenty of places to visit. They always stopped for lunch and thoroughly enjoyed their day.

On one of these trips, Charlie got down on one knee and asked Mary if she would marry him. Charlie had been carrying a solitaire diamond ring in his pocket for weeks and had not dared to ask her. Mary was taken aback as she knew Charlie liked her but did not think he would marry again after losing his wonderful wife. Mary said, "Are you sure?"

Charlie laughed and answered, "Of course I am, I have loved you for a while and thought you were just looking for friendship, but I decided to take the chance and ask you to marry me. Mary, you have made me the happiest man alive. I never thought I could feel the way I do for you, especially after losing my wife Hilda. I cannot wait to have you as my wife, I will promise to look after you, care for you, and try to be the best husband ever. Of course, if you will have me?"

Mary replied, "Charlie I have fallen in love with you, the way you treat me is exactly the kind of husband I would wish for. I also promise to look after you and care for you as a loving, faithful wife." Laughingly, she said, "When are we going to get married?"

Charlie told her, "How about yesterday?" They both hugged each other and laughed.

Mary teased him, "Are you going to put that ring on my finger then?" They were just so elated; nobody or nothing could spoil their mood.

Charlie and Mary got married at the end of the month in a small private ceremony. To celebrate, they enjoyed a meal at a charming hotel in Newcastle, accompanied by Charlie's brother and sister-in-law, who served as their witnesses.

Chapter Five
Charlie

Charlie was true to his word, and he was the most wonderful caring husband, anyone could wish for. Mary loved him and could not have asked for a better husband. Charlie even helped with the housework and washing up, he even helped with the cooking.

Of course, they had free goodies from Charlie's Butcher Shop, beef, lamb, pork, sausages, mince, black pudding, chicken, etc. Charlie loved cooking and made wonderful pies, stews, and roasts. They had quite a few friends who used to love to come round for dinner as they knew they were getting the best from Charlie's shop and of course Charlie and Mary's company, they were a lovely couple to be around and such good fun. So made for each other.

Every Sunday weather permitting, they went out in the car to somewhere new. Mary made up a picnic hamper for their day out. Sandwiches of corned beef and tomato, pease pudding and ham, or tinned pink salmon and cucumber. Two slices of cake, and a flask of tea. This was their special time together. They made a lot of happy memories.

One year, the Winter was the harshest on record in Newcastle. The snow was several feet deep and with the extremely low temperatures it froze. Charlie had to open his shop so that everyone could eat. Each morning, he made the journey to his shop in these hazardous conditions. What would normally be a 15-minute walk, took an hour due to the snow being two feet deep and frozen.

Although he was well wrapped up, he was shivering and wet by the time he got to the shop. Charlie had a set of dry clothes plus an apron hanging up in the back of the shop to change into. Afterward, he made himself a big mug of tea to help shake off the chill—he was frozen to the bone.

Of course, a butcher's shop needs to be cold with the meats being kept in the cold cabinets, so he never really got warm.

Charlie was busier than expected, his regular customers facing the elements to buy a couple of sausages or slices of bacon. The housewives had to be careful and thrifty with their housekeeping money. So, a half pound of mince would have onions and carrots added to it to bulk it up plus some suet dumplings or mashed potato. This would feed a big family. If anyone were still hungry, a slice of bread and margarine would suffice.

Charlie was a generous man and often added a few more ounces to the mince without them knowing. If it were a family who has fallen into extremely demanding times with husband out of work and quite a few bairns to feed, Charlie would add in a few sausages, extra mince, and some extra trimmings from the meats to keep them going without them knowing. He was a caring, good man.

The extreme weather conditions lasted several weeks, and Charlie caught flu which turned into bronchitis, he was ill, but tried to get to his shop most days, it was a struggle, but he needed to be there for his customers and their families. Charlie's bronchitis got worse, and he took to his bed. Mary nursed him day and night constantly. Poor Charlie was getting worse. He developed pneumonia and sadly passed away.

Mary was totally devastated by Charlie's death. Not only had she lost the love of her life but her soulmate as well. Her faith was tested; she asked God *WHY!!!? Why take a good and caring man with a beautiful soul?* But then beautiful souls do go to heaven.

When Charlie became bedridden and had no chance of getting better, they discussed their finances and Wills. Charlie left absolutely everything to Mary. The only stipulation was that she distributed all his clothes to the neighbour's husbands. They did not have much and thought that they would be appreciated.

Mary carried out Charlie's wishes and her neighbours were so grateful to have such lovely clothes. If anything was too big, it was altered and and any spare bits of material were put into a sewing basket to go into the making of a "clippie mat" Every household had a clippie mat which usually went infront of the fire. These mats/rugs were made of a hessian backing where strips of material were pushed through with and knotted giving a "shaggy" look.

Irene Richardson

Chapter Six
Christmas

Mary became a bit of a recluse, and her health was failing too. Her neighbours and friends became worried about her state of mind as well and she became a bit depressed.

Grace's visits cheered Mary up no end, this wonderful, beautiful niece, who had such a tragic life herself. How could she be so cheery and take the time to visit her? Mary marveled at her strength and resilience and thought how tragic she herself must seem to everyone. It was enough to shock her back to a more normal life. Little did Mary know how deeply Charlie's death affected her and that she would not live for very much longer.

Mary was left everything in Charlie's Will. His money in the bank and his butcher's shop! Which would be put up for sale soon and the money that was already in the Bank was for Mary too.

It was Christmas, Byker was a poor area in Newcastle, where everyone just survived. The men either worked in the Coal mines, the Shipyard, or an engineering factory. Workers were usually paid off at Christmas time and re-employed after New Year to save the firm from paying holiday wages. This meant there was no extra money for Christmas. Yet, despite the hardships, the community looked out for one another. The housewives banded together to make sure everyone had enough to eat, a simple Christmas dinner.

The bairns had a Christmas stocking hanging on the fireplace on Christmas Eve. It was always a dad's woolen sock filled with an orange, apple, some monkey nuts, a small chocolate bar, and a penny down at the toe. They often did without themselves to get these for the young ones. It was such a struggle.

This Christmas Mary decided that she would do something nice for her neighbours and their bairns to have a special Christmas this year. She had money in the bank for a rainy day. Why not give these bairns a Christmas to remember?

She was friends with about six families who had between three and six bairns each. Mary had an idea to make up a Christmas stocking for their children. She made up a list of all the things she needed and two of the mothers volunteered to do the shopping.

Her list for each stocking was: 1 x apple, 1 x orange, 1 x banana, 1 x chocolate bar, some sherbet, a handful of monkey nuts, a bag of sweets, and a silver shilling.

Mary wanted to give them a toy wrapped up to open on Christmas morning too. Depending on their age, a doll, a post Office set, a box of colored pencils and colouring in a book, a football, skipping ropes, a snakes and ladders game, a wooden pull-along car, or an airplane.

On Christmas Eve, a few of the mothers and Mary sat around a roaring coal fire and wrapped the Children's presents. Mary gave them all a glass of sherry with a mincemeat pie.

As they drank their sherry, they thanked Mary profusely for their bairns' presents, and told her how kind, thoughtful, and generous she was, and they could not wait till morning to see their little beaming faces!

Mary also had a surprise present for all the nearby six neighbours who were her friends as well.

She had asked Grace, last time she was here to get 6 nice Christmas Cards, as she needed them for her neighbours.

Mary had enclosed a £5 note in each of them, Dotty, Aggie, Norma, Katy, Dorothy, and Lizzie as a thank you for all their help and looking out for her. She also had Grace wrap six bars of rose-scented soap as a special present for them. This was a true luxury in those days. For their husbands, six bottles of Newcastle Brown Ale each. This would be a Christmas to remember for them. The biggest surprise was that they had to pop into Charlie's butcher shop, which was still open, but a sale had been agreed with Mr. Harris for the New Year.

Waiting to be collected by the mothers early the next morning was a parcel holding a turkey with all the trimmings, sausages, bacon, stuffing, and a pot of gravy. Mary had also arranged for Mrs. Kell, the owner of the Fruit and Veg shop next door, to hand in a selection of potatoes, sprouts, carrots, green cabbage, and turnip to the turkey order.

The families would eat well this Christmas!

Without the help and generous support from these women, Mary did not want to think what would have been.

After her neighbours had gone, Mary sat in her armchair in-front of the roaring fire and sipped another Sherry. What a lovely night I have had wrapping the presents and having friends help her.

She had enough money to live comfortably and give these people a little bit of it, so why not? She smiled thinking about the bairns' faces as they emptied their woolly socks and opened their presents.

With a smile on her face, a couple of sherries drank and a roaring coal fire, she drifted off into a comfortable sleep. She dreamed of Charlie grinning at her looking ever so proud of what she had done.

There was a knock at the front door, which woke and startled her.

She had slept all night in her chair, it was Christmas morning.

Rubbing the sleep from her eyes, she hurried to answer the door. To her surprise, about 25 bairns stood outside, grinning from ear to ear!

One of the older ones piped up. "We just want to thank you for writing to Santa Claus to maybe bring us a present on Christmas morning and he did!" They were jumping up and down.

"Merry Christmas and thanks Mrs Charlie" and off they ran.

The plan had worked, the mothers would tell the little ones that Mary was going to write to Santa this year and tell him how good they were and to see if he could deliver a small present to them on Christmas morning. Mary was smiling from ear to ear, something she had not done since Charlie died. "Oh Charlie, if you could have seen their little faces, they were beaming! Mary had tears in her eyes to see the joy on those bairns' faces." Pull yourself together Mary, she told herself, better get ready for my Christmas Dinner next door, food courtesy of Charlie's Butchers!

She had made a Christmas pudding laced with brandy for the grown-ups and a strawberry trifle for the bairns. Basket packed with the puddings and a jug of creamy custard; off she went next door.

Mary had not been out since Charlie passed away and was a bit nervous about going, it was only next door she told herself, but she was so glad she made the effort as she had an amazing day with Dorothy and Alfie and their 4 bairns, Susan, David, Kenneth and Peter aged 3,4,5 and 6. Dorothy looked older than her young age, having 4 children one after another, but there was love in the family even though they didn't have much.

A Newcastle Lass

The bairns played Blind Man's Buff, Pin the Tail on The Donkey, and Snakes and Ladders which Peter had gotten off Santa. Alfie was a good singer and played the banjo, it was old with a string missing, but he was good, and everyone joined in,

Mary slept so well that night, the best in years, Bless you Santa Claus! and a special thank you to you Charlie for giving me the means to buy these presents, oh I really miss you, but know you will be looking down today and seeing the joy and happiness on these bairns faces. I could not have wished for a better day!

Irene Richardson

Chapter Seven
Confessions

Grace continued to visit Aunt Mary as much as she could. It was during one of these visits that Mary noticed some bruising on Grace's face and asked her about it.

"Grace, tell me what is happening between you and Henry, this is not the first time I have seen a bruise on you, but never said anything as I waited for you to tell me in your own time."

Grace opened and told Mary everything, Grace was shocked but not surprised. Henry had a reputation for the girls, having a short fuse and a bit of a temper. Not a good combination.

She had hoped that a nice girl like Grace would change him, but obviously not.

Mary gave Grace a five-pound note, "This is for you to keep safe for whatever reason and to help you, you do not have to stay with this man…. Choose the right time and leave."

"Thank you, Aunt Mary, I will."

She also told Mary that she was pregnant again. Mary hugged her and said, "All will be fine lass, be strong, I am a great believer in karma. There are people on this earth who do dreadful things, but they do not get away with it, it will catch up with them sometime, and they will get their comeuppance, be patient, my lovely niece, something will happen, and you will get all the happiness you deserve." They kissed goodbye and little did Grace know that it would be the last time she would see Aunt Mary.

As Grace's pregnancy continued, Henry was not as violent as usual, was he getting soft and perhaps the time was right to be a father?

It was during Grace's 8th month of pregnancy that Henry came home early from work, a scowl on his face, eyes red, and was truly angry!

Grace knew something serious had happened and tried to keep out of his way. Henry had lost his job, was fired for being drunk on several occasions, and had several warnings, but he did not take any notice. Now he had no job and no income. What was he to do?

"What is it, Henry? Tell me what is wrong?" This coming from his weak and groveling wife, was the fuel that lit his pent-up rage. He lunged for Grace and his fists took over giving way to all his anger and frustrations.

Grace tried to protect her unborn child. When Henry was exhausted, he fell into a chair and went to sleep having consumed several whiskies at the pub before he staggered home to this nightmare.

Grace could hardly stand; she hurt everywhere and found that she had blood between her legs. She howled as she crawled to the front door to get help from her neighbour who had heard what was going on.

The police officer was called and promptly arrested Henry, cuffed him, and took him to the cells at the nearby police station on Headlam Street to cool off.

Meanwhile, a midwife was contacted to tend to Grace. Even though the beating she suffered had a severe effect on her mind and body, she gave birth to a beautiful, healthy baby girl… Isabella.

As Grace looked down at her beautiful daughter's face, she vowed to give her the life she deserved, not the nightmare she had suffered at the hands of Henry, her dad. "Dad?" she thought… he does not know the meaning of it!

Aunt Mary had passed away just weeks ago, and Grace felt a huge overwhelming sadness that Mary would never see Isabella.

Aunt Mary had left Grace her house, all her belongings, and her savings for her to make a clean start. She had let Grace know of her intentions and provisions in her will previously so that she could at last get away from the monster she had married and have the kind of life she deserved.

Henry did not know about the current will, but he was made aware by Mary before she passed away, that her estate was to be given to her brother who lived in Ireland. So, there was to be no money, etc., left for Grace and him. A lie she needed to tell this man.

It was time to move on for him, try and find someone who had a few bob and be able to keep him and give him a comfortable life. A rich widow looking for a younger stud. Foolish old dears, but hey, at this stage in his life, he could shut his eyes and spend their money. An excellent situation where both sides got what what they wanted.

He had nothing now, no job, dependency on alcohol and cigarettes, and what is more, could not even afford a fumble with one of the local prostitutes down at the docks. He did not have enough money to pay for one. They told him to "get lost "He got into a violent rage and started to beat up one of the girls. Her pimp was having none of it and gave Henry a good going over. Someone found a Policeman and Henry was arrested for disturbing the peace and causing bodily harm.

Henry was sitting in the cold cell at the Police Station, feeling sorry for himself. What had he done to deserve all this? He was blind to his faults, and unfortunately was now starting to sober up, his head was throbbing, and to top it all, he had caught something from one of the ladies he had been with and was itching like mad around his private bits. Need to go to the doctors soon.

Henry would be out of there in the morning and would go and stay with his mate Robbie for a while until he decided what he was going to do.

Grace had not heard from Henry in over a week now, he did not know he had a daughter. Grace had decided that she was going to start a new life with her beautiful baby and that certainly did not include Henry... he could rot in hell forever. She had eventually seen him in all his rotten glory. He had thrived on dominating and terrorizing her, beating her whenever he pleased and belittling her until she believed she was worthless. Not anymore, Aunt Mary had provided the means to leave him and start to live the life she was meant to have with her new daughter, Isabella.

Chapter Eight
Unwanted Strangers

Aunt Mary's house had 3 bedrooms, and it was written in a letter that when Grace moved in, one other room was to be left to Mary's half-cousin's nephew Harry Fenton. He was a big and burly but kindhearted man.

He had just left the Army having served 7 years in Scotland and lodging at Mary's came just at the right time. Mary had explained about Grace and her Will to Harry in a letter a few months ago. He understood the position Grace would be in without Henry, and it would be his job to make sure she was safe and not bothered. Anyone facing up to Harry would either be very stupid or very brave. Harry was 6 ft 4 and was just as wide, any messing with him would be like punching a brick wall. He would stand no nonsense and would make sure Henry knew this and sling his hook or he may not live to tell the tale.

Grace moved into Avondale Road as agreed with her late Aunt Mary. Harry was settled in too. They got on well with each other instantly.

Things were going well, for Grace and her baby Isabella. There was laughter in the house and Isabella just smiled and gurgled every time Harry came in the room. He absolutely adored her.

Two months later...

For once in her life things were more peaceful for Grace. Her constant fear of Henry turning up was easing due to having Harry around.

He was a gentle giant of a man, kind and thoughtful too, what is more, he adored Isabella and would often offer to look after her to let Grace go to the shops for her messages. At first, Grace was unsure about going out on her own, always looking around for Henry. But later she found out that he had moved to Sunderland and was living with a rich widow.

What Grace did not know was that Aunt Mary had made a deal with Henry, that she would give him a large amount of money to move away and leave Grace in peace, it was an offer he could not refuse. He had no feelings for her or the baby, so why not?

Grace's divorce came through and finally, she was rid of this man who had made her young life a total nightmare.

Her mam and dad, James and Nora were part of her life once again. Though her father had not fully welcomed her back into the family yet, but his stubborn nature with old-fashioned ideas and principles, made it difficult for him to express his feelings. But secretly he had missed his beautiful daughter. And now, with the arrival of his precious granddaughter, he could not deny the bond forming. He chose to forget about her no-good father, Henry—after all, the baby was innocent in all of this.

Everything was looking good; Grace was happy now but was still wary of Henry turning up unexpectedly.

About six months later, she received a letter from a Mrs Donnelly. The postage stamp was from Sunderland; it turned out to be the rich widow that Henry had moved in with. She opened the envelope to discover that Henry had been killed in an accident whilst working in the Docks as a general labourer. A crane had accidentally dropped its load of concrete blocks and Henry and two other men who were working alongside the cranes had been killed instantly. The Company had paid compensation to the families of the three men. Mrs Donnelly thought it was only right that Henry's compensation money went to Grace and her daughter.

The sum of £500 was enclosed.

Grace could not believe that she was now completely rid of her ex-husband Henry who had robbed her of her youth and made her feel inadequate in every way. The beatings she had to endure often with no reason at all. The love two people shared was not something she ever knew. Looking back, was she honestly happy? The only good thing to come out of the last few years was her little daughter Isabella who was sleeping contentedly in her arms after having been fed.

Grace took her through to the bedroom, laid her gently in her cot, and tucked her in.

Harry would be home soon; he was having a couple of pints at the Raby Pub after work with a friend who was joining the army. The bar was busy with it being a Friday night. Wages had been paid. The conversations in the bar were about experiences in the Army.

The bang of the front door made Grace jump, it was just after six and starting to get dark, Grace wondered who was calling at this time of day.

She opened the door tentatively.

Standing at the door were two men whom she did not know. "Can I help you?" she asked.

One of the men replied, "We are friends of Harry I thought we'd look him up, we were in the forces together."

"Come in and wait for him he should be back any time now." She showed them through to the kitchen.

"Can I get you a cup of tea while you are waiting?" Grace offered them.

"No, you're all right Mrs, we just had a few pints in the local pub." Grace could smell, the beer on them, she thought they had drunk much more.

"How long have you known Harry?" inquired Grace.

The taller one answered, "We were mates in the army down on the South Coast where we were stationed together for a couple of years."

Grace thought this was strange as Harry was stationed in Scotland.

The smaller one said, "We had heard Harry, and you got some money as compensation for your husband's death and Harry owes us some money from his army days and we thought we would come and collect."

"How much does he owe you?" asked Grace.

"Fifty quid," said the tall one. "Perhaps you could give it to us now and we'll be on our way."

She hesitated and was about to run to the front door. He made a grab for Grace and twisted her arm up her back. "We don't want any trouble, where do you keep the money, hurry up, we don't want to hurt you, mind you, you are a pretty bit of stuff, what do you think Jamie?"

"Aye she's a looker alright," he remarked as he grabbed at Grace's blouse and ripped it down the front. "What have we here then, a lovely pair, want some Jamie?" Grace screamed, but they just told her to shut up, slapped her face, and held her down.

Just at that moment Harry came through the door, heard Grace's screams, and ran through to the kitchen and saw what was happening.

He was raging and went for the two men almost beating them to a pulp if it had not been for Grace shouting for him to stop. With one final shove, he threw the sorry pair out onto the street, where neighbours had gathered, drawn by the commotion. Some of the women kicked and punched the men and some spat on them. Shouts rang out: "Do not ever come around these parts again, or you will never live to tell the tale, now bugger off before we call the Polis!" The two guys ran as fast as they could before any of them changed their minds.

Grace was shaking with shock; Harry put his arms around her until she stopped sobbing. "What a fool I was Harry, I believed them and let them in, I only twigged something was not right when they said they were in the army with you stationed on the South Coast and you had spent your time in Scotland. If you had not come home at that minute, I hate to think what would have happened!"

"There, there, now pet, I do not think they will be back. I was talking to these blokes in the pub about an hour ago, they were also in the army. We were reminiscing about army life and how we are doing now. Jesus, I forgot about Isabella, is she ok, where is she? If anything has happened to her, I will not be responsible for my actions Grace."

"Calm down Harry, I had put her down to sleep in her cot and never heard a peep from her, I'll just make sure she is alright."

Harry let go of Grace and they both went into Grace's bedroom where Isabella was sleeping soundly. "Oh Harry, thank you for what you do for us, you are just such a kind and caring man." Grace went over to Harry and kissed him on the cheek. They both were surprised that the closeness felt so natural. It was Harry who pulled away first saying, "Right missus, what's for tea?"

Grace thought that he did not want a kiss or hug from her after all he was her lodger, she was a bit taken aback by his response but put it to the back of her mind and started to fry the kippers that had been bought fresh at the fishmongers on Shields Road. Harry loved Kippers.

Chapter Nine

Harry

For the next couple of weeks, they tried to avoid being close and kept their conversations lighthearted. Both Grace and Harry felt something of an attraction between them but did not know how the other person felt.

One night, as a special treat, they went out to the pub for a couple of drinks, and a kindly neighbour, Katy, babysat for them.

They walked home from the pub hand in hand, and it felt so natural.

Katy was sitting by the fire having a cup of tea when they arrived back. Grace asked Katy how Isabella was, and she replied. "She was as good as gold andhad been asleep since 7 o'clock. Well, I will just finish my cup of tea. Then I will be off home." Harry insisted on walking Katy home, although she only lived at the top of the road

However, at this time of night, you never knew if there were any idiots hanging about, so it was better to be safe than sorry.

Grace changed into her night dress and dressing gown just before Harry got back.

When Harry came back in, Grace took Harry's hand and led him to her bedroom.

Everything felt so natural as they made love for the first time. In the morning, when Grace woke up, she looked over at Harry. He was awake and had a huge grin on his face. "What are you smiling at?" asked Grace. Harry pulled her close to him and said, "Grace, I feel like the luckiest man in the entire world. I have loved you since the moment I saw you, and I would like to make an honest woman of you after what happened last night…," he chuckled, "will you marry me please?"

Grace smiled and said, "I'll think about it, Harry." Harry began to tickle her. "I'll give you something to think about," as he rolled her over and began to make love to her again.

Harry and Grace were married at the registrars in a small family ceremony, where Grace became Mrs Fenton.

They went back to Grace's parents' house for a small celebration meal with just a couple of close friends and family and, of course Isabella.

When they went into the Living Room, they got an amazing surprise. Her parents had contacted some of their old friends they had not seen for years, such as school friends, neighbo**urs** and family. They all had been waiting in the living room quietly, ready to surprise them. "Surprise," they all shouted.

Irene Richardson

Grace could not stop the tears from running like a stream down her face. She could hardly speak; Harry just cuddled her until she stopped.

Grace was in total shock for the rest of the afternoon! She had a wonderful time catching up with old friends and meeting a couple of Harry's army friends. Grace's parents had a huge buffet for everyone and a two-tier wedding cake as well.

They celebrated until the early hours of the morning. When the last guests had gone, Grace's Mam had made up her old bedroom. She had lovingly prepared Grace's old bedroom, transforming it into a romantic retreat. She had put flower petals on the bed, a bottle of champagne, and two glasses on the bedside table. The room looked beautiful!

Next morning, the wonderful smell of a cooked breakfast was calling them downstairs.

They got dressed quickly and went into the kitchen to find the table set with the best china. They all tucked into a full Englishbreakfast with lots of tea. The conversation was all about their wedding and could not thank Grace's parents enough for the most wonderful surprise. Isabella was only half listening as she was busy tucking into her lovely breakfast.

Harry turned to Grace and said, "Well Mrs.Fenton, I have one more surprise for you. I have booked a hotel in the Lake District for three nights for our honeymoon. Your Mam and Dad have kindly offered to look after Isabella. So, we are driving there this afternoon, so get your skates on, wife of mine; your case is packed and, in the car, so let us get going!"

For once, Grace was speechless but grinning from ear to ear.

They had a brilliant time in the Lake District, staying at a lovely hotel in Windemere.

They visited lots of towns nearby during the day and had their evening meal at the hotel each night.

It all passed by too quick, and they made the journey home feeling very rested and relaxed.

Once back home, it was back to reality, having had a wonderful wedding day and a honeymoon in the Lakes. This truly was an amazing time for them as a happy married couple/ family. Grace could not be happier than she was at this precise moment in her life.

"Good riddance to you, Henry, this is how you should treat a lady, and this is how happy a marriage should be. May you rot in hell for your sins," Grace said quietly and now she knew the true meaning of love between two people.

Irene Richardson

Chapter Ten
New Beginnings

Baby Robert was born in September. a beautiful baby with a mop of dark hair, just like his dad. He was a good baby, and his sister Isabella just adored him. Harry and Grace were perfect for each other, and just before the following Christmas, baby John was added their family. Their house in Avondale Road was not big enough for their growing family, so they decided to look for a bigger one.

They found a 4-bedroomed house in Walker, which was ideal for their needs. With a lick of paint, they could move in straight away. The carpets were of decent quality and with a good shampoo, they would be fine.

Moving day arrived, and all the neighbours rallied around to help. Handcarts, prams, go-carts, and everything that had wheels were used to transport all Harry and Grace's possessions.

By mid-afternoon, they were in their new home. It would take several days to put the place right. Their priority was the bairn's beds so that they could get their sleep. Some of their friends stayed on to help unpack the main things. Mrs. Biggs, a neighbour made a big pot of Lentil Soup for everyone, and Mrs. Ross had baked a couple of loaves of bread.

Grace was so thankful for all the help and gave them all a hug. "Aww, Bonny Lass it is no bother; that is what friends do. We are glad to help." They all tucked into their soup with a hunk of bread dipped in. Harry and Grace looked around at the people sitting on odd chairs, boxes, and the floor. They were sad that they were moving from their friends and neighbours, but this was a fresh start for them, and they were welcome to visit anytime.

Within weeks, the house had everything in place: carpets cleaned, curtains up, drawers, cupboards and pantry filled.

Harry and Grace were exhausted, but as they sat by the coal fire one night, bairns bathed and, in their beds, they smiled at each other, knowing they had done the right thing, and this was a fresh start for them. Grace silently thanked Aunt Mary for leaving everything to her when she passed away and thanked Mrs. Donaldson for the compensation money from Henry's employers. Times were changing.

Harry had been a timeserved apprentice and a draughtsman before he joined the army. After leaving the Army, he had started back in the same Drawing Office in the Engineering Factory about a year ago.

Irene Richardson

The head of the drawing office was Mr. Collins, who trained Harry over 8 years ago and they got on well together. Harry respected Mr Collins as he had taken the time and the patience to make sure Harry finished his apprenticeship with honors. When Harry applied for this current position, he had no hesitation in recommending him for the job.

There were only four draughtsmen in the drawing office, including Mr. Collins; there were 2 apprentices, Mick and Jamie and himself. Mick has only one year left, and Jamie had two years left. They were both good workers and produced very neat and precise drawings, and their calculations were spot-on.

Mr Collins was nearing retirement age and was hoping to retire in a couple of months. He spoke to Harry about this and said that he would like to recommend him to take over as Head of the Office. The two apprentices were more than capable of completing the work that the were given, with Harry just keeping an eye out and the final checking their work before it went into production. Mr. Collins said that he was going to see about starting a new apprentice straight from school. However, he would need to discuss the matter with head office before making any arrangements.

Harry was pleased that Mr Collins thought he could take over this very responsible job.

He knew he could do it, but just getting Mr Collins's recommendation for the job, meant a lot to him.

After a few weeks, Harry was summoned to head office to confirm his new status as head of the drawing office, which would start in two weeks' time when Mr. Collins retired. Mr Laidlaw, the Head of Staff Manager, said that they had advertised for a new apprentice and were getting letters from school leavers every day. He would like Harry to sit in during the interviews for his input.

Harry could not wait to get home and tell Grace the good news. His new salary would be a 10% rise for six months and then another 20% rise for the next year. After that, they would review the situation.

When Harry got home that night and told Grace about what had happened with his job and promotion, she was so pleased for him and told him he deserved it.

Baby Robert had just been bathed, and Harry sat on his knee and gave him his bottle of milk. He loved this time with his son. Isabella was playing in her room and heard Harry (whom she called daddy? She never knew about her real dad, Henry) came running up to him, climbed up on his other knee, put her arms around his neck and gave him a big kiss on the cheek. Harry said to her, "Hello my poppet, you been a busy girl today?"

"Yes Daddy," she said, and "I have been good too."

"Well," said Harry, if you reach into my pocket, you will find something there which is only for a good girl. There was a little bar of chocolate in there for her. She squealed with delight and ate it all up quickly.

Grace saw what happened and said, "I hope you do not have a sore tummy; little miss anyway. It is time to get your nightie on and ready for bed. When you have done that, I have a cup of warm milk for you." Robert and John were settled down for the night. Isabella always went to bed half an hour later.

John, Robert, and Isabella were good children. Harry just adored them. He had a wonderful wife Grace, who was his world.

Harry sat in his chair feeling very contented. He thought about his life now and nodded off to sleep with a huge smile on his face.

Grace came back into the living room after putting the bairns to bed and saw Harry asleep in the chair. She crept into the kitchen to finish making his dinner. She was making shepherd's pie, which was his favourite. Harry woke up as he smelled the wonderful pie." Grace, he said, "I am such a lucky man, and all this has happened since the day I met you. I love you, Grace so much I just wanted to tell you before I fell asleep again! And missed my Shepherd's Pie." Grace punched his arm, laughing and gave him a big kiss.

Harry just loved overseeing the drawing office; he made sure that the apprentices Mick and Jamie got a little bit more responsibility over time, which led to more experience. He gave them both some challenging work, and they completed the drawings and calculations brilliantly. Harry made sure they had praise for the work as Mr Collins had done for him as an apprentice. Richard, the new apprentice, was very funny and kept everyone laughing. He was picking up the tasks that were set for him with no problem. He was a bright lad, and Harry knew he had the makings of a good Draftsman one day.

One morning, when Grace had finished breakfast, Isabella was at school, and Robert and John were going out for-the day with her Mam and Dad. Harry had gone to work early as usual, she felt a little lightheaded and had an upset stomach. Think I have been doing too much. She thought. I will just sit by the fire with a cup of tea for a little while, which she did. After about 10 minutes, she was feeling worse and had to run to the sink and was sick. Grace knew the symptoms well and thought she was pregnant, but she was not sure how she felt having another baby. John went to the mother and toddlers' group 3 mornings a week; Robert was at the Infants School, and Isabella would be starting at the junior school after the Summer Holidays. Did she really want another baby?

Grace thought about it all day; she decided just to see how it panned out. she would not mention this to Harry until she was sure it could be a false alarm; she would need to wait.

Grace was right; it was a false alarm. She would not tell Harry though; there was no need to have him upset when he was just so happy, something she had not seen since she had met him.

Irene Richardson

Chapter Eleven
Mother and Toddler Group

Over the next few years, their children were growing up. Isabella was at the Junior School on Welbeck Road. She was going into the Seniors next year.

She was a beautiful child, and now even more beautiful as a teenager with a sunny nature. She never lacked for friends and was always bringing home a friend or two after school. Grace did not mind this at all. The girls used to look after Robert and John, and she was given a chance to make tea in peace. Although she loved all her children, Grace sometimes felt that her life was spent at home with them, doing all the household chores etc., with no time for herself.

It was one Sunday after the service at St Michael's Church; she was talking to the vicar, Mr Anderson, about an idea she had that would help the community and make use of St. Michael's Hall.

Grace had thought of bringing together the mothers who, like her, were at home all day with the little ones. It would be quite a long day with just the children, like Grace, something for herself, so what about a mother and Toddler Group in the hall a couple of times a week? This would be company for the women; they would make new friends, and the little ones could play with one another. Mothers could take it in turn to supervise the children, and they could have a cup of tea. There was a kitchen in the hall, so no problem with the refreshments.

Mr. Anderson thought that would be a great idea Would Grace like to organize and set it up? Of course, there would be a small fund from the Church available to cover the setup.

Grace could not wait to get home to tell Harry the good news. He was delighted to hear about her plan and offered to make and print some notices to hang on some lampposts around the neighbourhood welcoming mothers to the Byker and Walker Mothers Group.

Grace and some of her neighbours collected books and toys for the babies and small bairns to play with. The hall had a good supply of cups and mugs as well as a hot water urn for tea making.

Opening Day arrived; Grace and a couple of her friends, Sarah, and Doris, were there to help and set up.

Grace was anxious, would anyone come along? 9 o'clock came, and so did around twenty women and their youngsters, eager to be a part of this new adventure.

One of the Mam's was a lovely young girl called Amy; she originally came from Scotland. She had a lovely, soft Scottish accent. She had met a young Welshman (who was a Carpenter to trade) who was working on a contract in Edinburgh. They met by chance in Princes Street Gardens. It was a beautiful sunny day, and they were both sitting on the same bench, eating their lunch. A conversation sparked, and from that moment, they were drawn to each other. They hit it off straight away and, after a long-distance relationship, married and moved to Newcastle with his job. They had a baby boy called Taran (Welsh for thunder).

Amy and Grace became close friends, and Amy was a

godsend helping with the Group She had lots of ideas and was a bundle of energy.

Amy's husband Rhys was starting a new job in Wales in a month's time, and they were to pack up and move there permanently. On Amy's last day at the group with Taran, the other mams had collected some money together and bought Amy a tea set as a leaving present. She was overwhelmed; how thoughtful, she only had a few old mugs.

Grace hugged Amy and Taran; oh, she would sorely miss them!!

The mother and toddler group was extremely popular within a few months, and word was beginning to spread. Soon, some other areas latched onto the idea and formed their own group.

Within a year of opening, there were another 5 groups that had taken on Grace's idea and opened a playgroup in their area.

Extra funds were always needed for new toys, books, and drinks.

All the mothers were on a tight budget, so Grace had a meeting with some to discuss this. So, it was unanimously decided that they would have a Spring Fair.

Donations were overflowing; everyone gave what they did not need.

A doll, an old three-wheeler bike, toy cars, some homemade cakes and biscuits, scones with raisins, homemade jam etc. Everyone had contributed whatever they could afford or did not have use for any longer.

The day of the fair arrived; everyone came to help set up.

Tables set, everyone manning their allocated stall; Grace could not believe how the hall looked. Time to let the crowd in.

It was a chaotic situation, with women rushing to buy things they needed for their homes. Someone went past Grace carrying a tin bath with a small hole in it, suppose it could be repaired.

When it was all over, there was absolutely nothing left. Grace was overwhelmed by how successful it had been and thanked everyone for contributing. They made more money than expected; th fair was a tremendous success.

The Mother and Toddler Group went from strength to strength, and as other groups were formed in the neighboring areas, it was a lifeline to a lot of mams and bairns to be able to meet new friends, to socialize and their offspring to interact with others a few times a week. The children got to play with a variety of toysthat they did not have at home.

Grace decided to pass over the management of the club to Sarah and Doris, who were more than capable of managing it.

This would give her more time at home, but she said if they needed her, to please get in touch, and she would be more than happy to come in and help.

Chapter Twelve
Isabella

"Mam, is it okay if I go to Janet's house for tea after school?" asked Isabella. Her mam is making mince and dumplings and jam sponge pudding. Can I please? I will be home by 8. Promise!

Grace looked at her daughter; how could she refuse when it had obviously been arranged beforehand between the pair?

"Of course, you can go, Pet, as long as you're home by 8:00 at the latest, and make sure you and Janet do your homework first."

Isabella jumped up and kissed her Mam on the cheek, "Thanks Mam, love you." And with that, she went off to school.

Grace suddenly realized that her daughter was a young teenager now and had her own friends. She suddenly felt old.

Isabella was an outgoing, bubbly girl and had several friends. Some of the boys at school really fancied Isabella but she was not interested in them. Isabella was having a fun time with her friends. There would be plenty of time for boyfriends. Robert was a popular child at school and was good at sports... He became captain of the football team. John was the bookworm type, and you could always find him in the library.

The next couple of years passed quickly, and before Grace knew it, Isabella was a young woman about to leave school and start her first job.

Isabella had not wanted to go into an office as some of her friends were doing, but she enjoyed meeting people. So, it was decided she would apply for a job as a counter assistant in Fenwick's Store, An upmarket retail store in the city centre.

Isabella went for an interview and got a job behind the counter as an assistant for Cyclax Perfumes and Cosmetics. Isabella completed the training course and gained an A + for the Exam she took. She was so excited to start work, as she loved meeting people and chatting with them, and she was ready for this!

Isabella worked 5 and a half days a week, Monday to Friday full time, and the store closed at one on a Saturday.

She was now 17 and had turned into a beautiful, eye-catching young woman. Attracting many wolf whistles wherever she went.

When she walked home each night, she always saw this one guy who caught her attention, he smiled at her. After a few weeks, he got into conversation with her, and they walked home over Byker Bridge. She found out that he lived not too far away from her in Middle Street. His name was Tommy Taylor. Isabella liked him straight away and found him to be a real gentleman and easy to have a good relationship with. Being the gentleman that he was, he walked Isabella home right to her front door to be on the safe side. As Tommy said, you could never be sure who was about looking for trouble these days. Isabella did feel safe with him.

She started to have feelings for Tommy, or was it just a teenage crush?

On a walk home one night, Tommy picked up the courage to ask Isabella if she would like to go out on a date with him one weekend, and she said yes.

Tommy Taylor worked at a big engineering factory on the lathe and grinding machines. He had been there since leaving school. He had learned his trade as an apprentice for 5 years, starting at age 15 and was now 23 years old.

He was now earning double the number of wages since his first day of starting. He learned quickly and well before his apprenticeship was finished. He had his own lathe machine and was also setting jobs up himself instead of the supervisor. At this rate he would have a supervisor's job soon.

Tommy was looking forward to his date with Isabella, but he could not believe his luck. She was a beauty, intelligent, had a decent job, and lived in a good area of Newcastle. As much as he was excited, a small part of him wondered if he was genuinely good enough for her. He was just a working-class man, had a decent job in a factory, and lived with his Mam and Dad in a terraced house in Walker.

Must be his good looks, he chuckled to himself.

Saturday came, and Tommy was really looking forward to seeing Isabella again. He had arranged to meet her outside the local Dance Hall at 7 o'clock. He had asked his mam to wash his best white shirt to wear. He decided to go to the Barbers for a hair cut that morning. Usually, it was his dad who cut the family's hair; he was good at it, but Tommy wanted to impress Isabella.

Tommy was feeling nervous waiting for Isabella outside the Dance Hall.

He was there at 6.45. Pacing up and down, hoping she would turn up and not change her mind.

He need not have worried as he saw her about 20 yards away walking towards him.

"Hello Tommy, have you been waiting long?" Isabella asked. "About 10 minutes... You do look lovely tonight, Isabella, that blue really suits you."

"Thanks, I love blue, it is my absolute favourite. Shall we go in? I am really looking forward to it."

The band was playing on stage, and Tommy and Isabella found a space on the dance floor and started to dance to a Waltz. It felt good to hold her close. She really smelled nice, sort of roses and lilies of the valley. He commented on her perfume. It was a Cyclax one called La Cinquieme Nuit (Fifth Night), a new one which she bought with her staff discount. So glad Tommy liked it.

Tommy was a good dancer, and he whisked Isabella around the dance floor with such ease that she felt really at home with him.

They both loved dancing and were on the floor every dance except a break for a drink.

On the way home, Tommy bought them some battered Haddock and Chips with a good helping of salt and vinegar from the local Chip Shop, which they ate with their fingers on the walk home.

At Isabella's front door, Tommy kissed her goodnight and walked back home. He had strong feelings for her and did not want to scare her off by coming on too strong. He hoped she felt something for him; time would tell.

Grace and Harry were waiting up for Isabella to make sure she had gotten home safe and asked about her date with Tommy.

"Oh, Dad and Mam, he is just so lovely and a perfect gentleman; you will love him. She then went on to tell them all about the date before yawning and going off to bed with a smile on her face, hoping to have dreams of him.

Irene Richardson

Chapter Thirteen
Tommy

Isabella just loved her job at the Cyclax Counter in Fenwick's and would give advice to customers who came to her counter. She also got an allowance for herself, which included a 10% staff discount on purchases and was allowed to do her own makeup from the tester displays before the store opened. A Peony Rose Perfume was bought for her mam out of her First Pay Packet. After all, her mam deserved a treat!

One day, not long after she had been out with Tommy, she had a visit from Tommy's **mam** at her counter. She said that Tommy talked about her all the time, so she would pop into Fenwick's to say hello the next time she was in town. They chatted away for ages as the store was not busy. Isabella liked Tommy's mam a lot; she was so easy to talk to, just like Tommy.

Tommy's Mam said she must come around for tea.... what about Sunday afternoon? Isabella said she would love that, so it was arranged for next Sunday, how nice that would be. She had a lovely time and got on so well with Tommy's mam and dad. They were lovely, warm, friendly people. They thought Isabella was really a lovely girl, and Tommy had gotten a good one there!

Isabella settled into her job nicely. It was a pleasure to get up in the morning and get ready for a new day at her counter at the store. Plus, all the lovely people she met throughout the day.

Although Isabella was kept busy at her work and had wonderful parents, a lot of her friends had been married at just 17 and either lived with their parents temporarily or were renting if they could afford to.

Isabella, who was 18 and almost ready to build a future with a nice man, but who with… Tommy was a definite maybe… not met anyone else yet, she thought. Isabella could not wait for the day when she was married and had her own place, but she would be patient. In the meantime, she was enjoying herself as a teenager, and life was good.

Isabella continued to see Tommy regularly and found she was really falling for him. He was a lovely, levelheaded man who was tender and caring.

One Sunday afternoon, Tommy took Isabella on the train to Whitley Bay. They walked along the front and even had a paddle in the cold, North Sea. They warmed up with a pot of tea and some egg sandwiches at a café near the beach, a lovely finish to their day. There were some tables and chairs outside, and they sat at one and watched the hustle and bustle of people on the beach promenade. They both agreed what a wonderful day they had.

It was time to catch the last train back to Newcastle, and they did not want to miss that, so they needed to hurry. Tommy and Isabella ran all the way to the Station, laughing and out of breath as they just managed to get on it with seconds to spare.

They strolled hand in hand back to Isabella's house. At the gate, Tommy kissed her and then went down on one knee with a ring in his hand. "Isabella, I love you with all my heart. Will you marry me?" Isabella gasped, caught completely off guard. She had not expected this—not so soon. Isabella looked at Tommy, still on one knee and thought, I could not do any better than spend the rest of my life with this wonderful and loving man. She was in love with him, so why hesitate? "Tommy, I love you too, and yes, I will marry you."

Tommy gave out a whoop of delight… oh Isabella, you had me going there, come here, and let me put this ring on your finger before you change your mind.

They hugged and kissed each other.

"Let's go and tell your dad and mam right now," said Tommy.

"Ok do not think they have gone to bed yet," Isabella replied, knowing that her parents would be peeking out one of the windows!

Grace and Harry were in on this secret and knew what Tommy had planned as he had asked Harry's permission to propose to

Isabella. In fact, they were peeping from behind the curtains in the front room.

Just as Isabella had imagined them to be doing!

It was decided that they would marry in June. Grace said she would be happy to make all the arrangements if they wanted. Tommy and Isabella thought it was an excellent idea as Grace was brilliant at organizing everything to the last detail.

Their wedding was to be held in Saint Michael's church in Byker on the 6th of June. Invitations were written and sent out to family and friends on both sides.

A dressmaker in Jesmond was to make Isabella's dress, her two bridesmaids and Grace's outfit. Isabella's dress was made of ivory silk and lace and was accompanied by a long train. Her bridesmaids, Ella and Janets' dresses were to be in pale blue silk. Grace chose a pale pink silk dress with a matching jacket with tiny rosebuds around the collar.

She found a pink pillbox hat to wear from a Milliners in Newcastle, a perfect match!

The men would wear a navy suit with a pale blue silk tie and a pocket handkerchief to match. The bouquets would be in pale pink, roses and white gypsophilas.

The wedding breakfast was to be held in Saint Michael's Hall next to the church.

Irene Richardson

They were to be 100 guests. The tables were set out and covered in white linen tablecloths. Down the centre of each table were small vases holding pink roses

Grace, with the help of her friends, did all the catering themselves, a huge task. Everyone had their part to play, and all went to plan.

It was decided that a buffet-style meal would be best, given the large number of guests and the warm June weather. A buffet table was set up at one end of the hall and was covered in mountains of food such as bowls of salad leaves with tomatoes, cucumbers, radishes, sliced onion rings, plates of boiled ham slices and other cold sliced meats, ham and egg, pie, cheese and onion, pie, pickled onions, beetroot, and pickles. Whole-boiled eggs sliced into salad cream. Several plates of sandwiches with different fillings, several baskets of bread. There was a table to the side which held puddings and bowls of chopped fresh fruit salad and trifles, some with sherry in them and others contained no alcohol. Several jugs of cream at the side.

There was a round table and stand for the wedding cake, a beautiful threetiered iced cake with pink roses and a bride and groom on top. Ready to be cut later.

Another table nearby was set up as a bar with bottles of beer and spirits, such as Whiskey, Rum, Brandy, Sherry and Port and juice for the non-drinkers and the bairns. There were all types of glasses.

A Newcastle Lass

In the church, the guests gathered, all dressed in their finery. Tommy was at the front with his best man, Sydney. Tommy was nervous as he waited, but not as nervous as Sydney, who kept checking his pocket for the wedding rings and a copy of his speech.

The organ started to play, and Isabella started to walk down the aisle on her dad's arm. Tommy turned around to watch her walk towards him. She looked like an angel and was so beautiful that it took his breath away. He had to wipe the tears away with his handkerchief. He thought to himself he must be the luckiest man in the world to be marrying this beautiful woman.

After the ceremony was over and photos were taken, the bridal party moved next door to the Church Hall for the wedding breakfast. The guests marveled at the display of buffet food and drinks table. The speeches from Isabella's dad, the best man and Tommy were all good in their own way. Harry's speech was sentimental about losing a much-loved daughter but getting a new son-in-law into the family and a special mention for Grace and her friends for doing such a marvelous job of the buffet. Everyone cheered.

The best man's speech was hilarious, and everyone was in fits of laughter with embarrassing tales about Tommy, as well as his warm wishes to the couple for a long and happy marriage.

Tommy was last to speak; he thanked parents, bridesmaids, and best man for all their help. Turning to Isabella, he said how beautiful she looked today and said lots of romantic words about being the luckiest man, etc.

Everyone toasted the Bride and Groom. Everyone was then invited to help themselves to the wedding breakfast, which they all thoroughly enjoyed. They thanked Grace for all her hard work. The Wedding Cake was cut.

Time now for the dancing to start. Tommy had hired the Kenny Milton Swing Band; he grew up with Kenny, and there was no better Band in Newcastle than this one.

The first dance for Tommy and Isabella was a slow waltz to one of their favourite songs. All the guests joined in after this, and they all had a marvelous time.

Even the older folk got up and had a dance but had to keep sitting down with aches and pains and out of breath that comes with age. But after a couple of sips of sherry, they were back on their feet, dancing once more!

When it was time for Tommy and Isabella to leave, the guests formed an arch for them, cheering them (and covering them in confetti). A car was parked outside and was waiting to take them to their hotel for the night.

Tommy and Isabella were just beaming. They had just the most amazing day.

Chapter Fourteen
Lord and Lady Park

Tommy had booked a room at a posh hotel in Jesmond to spend their Honeymoon night, and Harry, who did not drink had offered to drive them to the hotel. And he would pick them up in the morning after breakfast.

They checked in at the reception and got the key to their room. When they found their room on the first floor of the hotel, Tommy picked up Isabella in his arms to carry her across the threshold. They were both nervous but happy too. "My word, Mrs. Taylor, you weigh a ton with all that food you have just eaten." Isabella slapped his shoulder, "Cheeky beggar," and kissed him.

The room Tommy had booked was the bridal suite, and Isabella gasped as she saw the beautiful room. It had a four-poster bed with ivory bedding, there was a chaise lounge in ivory floral tapestry in the bay window. Deep piled carpets in pale blue and curtains in the same colour.

A dressing table with a mirror on one wall. Two blue floral tapestry covered armchairs with a small table in front of them which had a silver tray on it. There was a silver tray with a bottle of Champagne in an Ice Bucket and two crystal glasses waiting to be filled. A note from the Management wishing them Congratulations was tied to the bottle of champagne with a tray of mints and chocolates at the side.

Isabella was speechless, eyes wide as she took it all in.

Tommy still had her in his arms.

"Nothing but the best for my new wife." He put her down, and she kissed him.

"Tommy, thank you. I have never seen anything so grand in my life."

They had their champagne, "First time for everything Isabella, let's get ready for bed," and gave her a cheeky wink!

"What about the chocolates, Tommy?"

"Let us save them for home. I could not eat another thing," said Tommy. He had more important things on his mind right now.

Isabella was feeling extremely nervous as she and Tommy had not gone past the kissing stage. Isabella was shy about undressing, but Tommy was very tender and gentle with her as he helped take off her wedding dress and finally her undergarments. Isabella folded her arms around her to cover her nakedness, but Tommy told her how beautiful she looked and held her close. He quickly undressed as well. They held each other for a while, and Tommy gently laid Isabella on the bed. He made love to her and was surprised by her passion. They slept for a while, and it was Isabella who woke

Tommy up and started to kiss him again. In his sleepy state, he was thinking, that the lovemaking side of their marriage was not going to be a problem.

"Right, my new wife, time to get some clothes on, otherwise I might be tempted to miss breakfast," Tommy said with a smile and a cheeky wink.

They got ready and went downstairs to the Dining Room, which was already busy.

The uniformed staff quietly rushed about looking after their guests very efficiently.

The dining room manager met them at the door, "Good morning, Mr. and Mrs. Taylor. I hope you both slept well and found the room satisfactory and comfortable."

Isabella blushed. "I have your table ready for you, if you would just follow me, please."

He showed them to a table for two which was in the Bay Window and overlooking Jesmond Dene, with a beautiful view of the trees and the river. It was perfect.

As they were looking at the Breakfast Menu, Tommy noticed the couple sitting at the table next to him. They were well dressed and looked as though they dined here often. The man who was facing Tommy kept staring at him. He looked familiar, but Tommy thought that he would not keep the company of these kinds of upperclass people.

The waiter went to the couple's table and said, "Are you ready to order Lord and Lady Park?"

Lady Park nodded. "I'll have the Eggs Benedict with a rasher of bacon on the side, croissants, and a strong coffee."

Lord Park glanced at the menu one last time. "The Full English with toast and strong tea for me."

With a polite nod, the waiter took their order and headed to the kitchen.

The gentleman, Lord Park, began to stare at Tommy again, he then began to walk to Tommy and Isabella's table.

"What is he wanting?" thought Tommy.

"It is Tommy Taylor from Byker, isn't it? he asked. Tommy was confused; 'how did a Lord know him?' He just nodded.

"I am Lord William Park. Way back last February, I was walking back to my car, which was parked on the quayside. As I walked along, a couple of young hooligans were cycling on their bikes extremely fast, and they knocked into me. It was very slippery, and I lost my footing and fell into the Tyne. You saved my life that day as you had no hesitation in jumping in.

"When I came round, you had disappeared. I asked some of the people standing there who you were, and one lady said, "That's Tommy Taylor from Byker. I wanted to thank you for what you did, but did not know how to contact you, but I never forgot your face, Tommy.

"So, a year and a half later, thank you Tommy Taylor, for saving my life."

"Will you both come and join Eleanor and I for breakfast?"

"I could not just do nothing in the circumstances, everyone was just standing and watching. So, I jumped, the water was bloody freezing, so I got you out quickly. I did not hang around because I was soaking wet and needed to get dry quickly. There were plenty of folk on the quayside to help you, so I shot off. And thank you for the invite for breakfast, but me and Isabella here just got married yesterday, and we need to get back home after breakfast as I must be at work tomorrow."

At that moment, Lady Eleanor came to the table, "Congratulations on your marriage. I hope you have a long and happy one. William and I have been married for 26 happy years; well sometimes he is a pain in the ass!" Isabella had to hide a giggle at that one, "But thank you so much for saving him; I don't know what I would do without the old bugger!" She winked and went back to the table as the waiter had just brought her breakfast.

"She could not stand cold food," Lord William said. He also told "Congratulations" to them and thanked Tommy once more for what he did and went to enjoy his Full English breakfast with strong tea.

"You never told me that," said Isabella. "Saving a Lord no less from drowning in the freezing River Tyne! You are daft, Tommy Taylor; you could have drowned too!"

The waiter came to take their order. Isabella had looked at Lady Eleanor's Eggs Benedict.

She figured she might never get another chance to eat like a Lord and Lady, so she decided to indulge. She ordered the same breakfast, along with croissants and tea.

"Strong, please," she added, determined to savor the full experience.

Tommy ordered the Full English breakfast: toast and "strong tea" as well. He wondered what "strong tea" was like. He just made it normally—tea was just tea—what would be the difference?

He would soon find out.

After breakfast was finished, they went back to their room to pack, not that they had much; one small suitcase held all their clothes. They sat in the window seat for a while and looked out at the scenery. Tommy said, "Isabella, if I had lots of money, I would treat you to all this on a regular basis. You deserve it; you are My Lady Isabella Taylor."

"Tommy, yer daft fool, I am happy the way we are. I love you for who you are and not what you are. Do not change a thing, and it is not every day you get to marry a real-life hero!"

Down at the reception, Tommy handed in the key and asked for their Bill. The receptionist said, "There is no charge Sir. Lord and Lady Park have paid your Bill and left this envelope addressed to you both.

Tommy opened the envelope, and a letter inside read:

"To Tommy and Isabella, many congratulations on your marriage; may it be as happy as mine and Eleanor's. Please accept this gift as a wedding present from us to buy something for your home. I would like to thank you again for your courageous and prompt saving of me from drowning last year on the River Tyne. I am so indebted to you for this unselfish act of bravery. I have paid for your room as you will have gathered as a huge thank you. You are an incredibly special person, Tommy. If you need anything in your life, please do not hesitate to contact me for any help I can give you. Kindest regards to your beautiful new wife, Isabella. Eleanor, and I wish you both every happiness for your future."

William and Eleanor Park,

Tyneside Manor,

Ponteland, Northumberland.

Tommy then opened the envelope and inside was a £100 note.

"Isabella, look, I have never seen one of these in my life! Oh, my goodness, he need not have done that. I only did what anyone would do."

"No, you did not Tommy! Everyone stood and watched, and you are the one who risked your own life to save him. I am so proud of you."

They were being picked up in her dad's car at 10.30. and he was parked outside.

Chapter Fifteen
Parker Street

Tommy had rented a two bedroomed terrace house in Parker Street and had been decorating and getting it up to scratch for a couple of months before the wedding as a surprise for Isabella. Her Mam and Dad were in on the secret and helped as well. Harry was handy with D. I.Y. and was extremely happy to get involved. Grace was the one with the vision| She sourced out the furnishings, knowing her daughter's taste.

They had worked secretively right through until a couple of days before the wedding. The house looked so fresh and clean; it was a good start for them, and so hard not to let the secret out.

Isabella was led to believe that she would be moving into her Mam and Dad's house to start their married life before they could afford their own house.

Tommy blindfolded Isabella explaining he had a surprise for her.

He put her next to him in the back seat, "no sneaking a peep." Harry had an old car, which he loved. He could afford a newer one,

A Newcastle Lass

but the car never let him down, he was fond of the old girl. He called her Beth. They set off to No. 85 Parker Street, Byker.

Tommy led Isabella by the hand to the newly painted blue door and took off her blindfold. He placed the keys in her hand, saying, "Welcome Home, Mrs. Taylor."

Isabella was absolutely dumbfounded; she could not speak. "Go ahead and open the door," said Tommy.

Isabella opened the door and went into the hall. It smelled of fresh paint. There was a long runner down the hall to protect the Lino underneath. Just past the front door was a door to a small bedroom with two single beds and a chest of drawers. The walls were painted pale blue, and there were curtains with tiny blue flowers. There was Lino on the floor and a blue rug between the beds.

"Oh Tommy, this is just beautiful, I don't know what to say." Tears were rolling down her cheeks.

"Come on Bonny Lass, let's see the rest!" Isabella followed Tommy to the end of the hall through a door which was the Living Room. The first thing she noticed was the big cast iron fireplace with a coal fire burning. The walls were decorated with a pale green, and the Lino on the floor was a deeper shade of green. There was a clipped rug in front of the fire made with assorted colors of greens and browns. A sofa and two armchairs in dark green and a half-glass walnut cabinet with two cupboards were on one wall. One wall held a large walnut framed clock with a brass pendulum ticking away, and as if it knew she had come into the room chimed 11 times for 11 o'clock as if to welcome her.

Isabella had tears of joy running down her cheeks. Tommy went to cuddle her. "You've still got to see the scullery and our bedroom Pet." The scullery walls were painted a sunny lemon color with a pale green lino floor. There was a stone sink, drainer, and bench down one side with a small window looking onto the backyard. It had yellow flowered curtains hanging on it. On the other wall was a gas cooker and a kitchen cabinet in pale green. The front cabinet opened into a small table, and Isabella's mam had baked a cake for them and beside it was two China cups and saucers, two small plates, a teapot, a milk jug, and a sugar bowl to welcome them to their new home.

Isabella stood frozen, completely speechless as she took it all in. "And last of all, Issy, is our bedroom." Tommy took her back into the living room, which had a door in the corner; this was their bedroom. Isabella started to cry all over again when she saw it had been decorated in her favorite pale blue. A lovely double bed with a pale blue chenille cover and bedside cabinets on either side. A dressing table and mirror and a double wardrobe for her as well. A Silver backed mirror Comb and Brush lay on top of the dressing table.

"Well do you like it?" asked Tommy. All Isabella could do was to hug him tightly as she soaked his coat with tears of joy.

"So, I take it that means 'Yes'?" He laughed.

As they were sitting having their tea and cake in front of the fire, Tommy confessed to his new wife about how, over the last few months, he said he had been working overtime, but that was an excuse to renovate the house with the help of some friends and her Mam Dad. They settled in straight away; Tommy had done a wonderful job of redecorating carpeting and furnishings. Isabella thought that her Mam had put a lot of thought and effort into getting it simply perfect!

Isabella continued to work at Fenwick's until she found out that she was pregnant, she handed in her notice before she was showing. She could now plan for the birth of her baby. Her Mam and Dad were delighted at the news and offered to buy a pram for the baby. Tommy's parents were so happy, too and they said they would pay for the baby's cot.

Isabella had time on her hands now; she was not working, so she set about knitting baby clothes and blankets. The chest of drawers in the front bedroom was getting full of clothes and blankets she had knitted. Plus, some nappies and a soft baby hairbrush. She bought a little item each week. It was a start.

Tommy did a few extra shifts at his work to get extra money for the baby when he or she arrived. When he eventually finished his work after doing overtime, Tommy was so exhausted he sometimes fell asleep after his tea in front of the fire.

One night, as they were sitting by the fire, Isabella asked Tommy what he would like to call his son or daughter.

"Well, I like Alexander for a boy and Mary Ellen for a girl said Tommy. What about you, Isabella...?"

"Well, I like Mary Ellen, but I think if it is a boy, we could call him Thomas after you."

"Tommy Junior sounds good, Isabella, I like that."

Isabella got her wish, and baby Thomas Junior was born in February in the middle of the night. The midwife had been called, but she arrived too late. Isabella gave birth with the help of a neighbour. The birth was quite easy, with no complications.

Isabella gave birth to a beautiful baby boy. He was a healthy boy weighing in at 9 lbs 6 oz, quite a big baby, considering Isabella was quite small. 'Hope he will fit his clothes,' went through her mind! Thomas hugged Isabella. He had tears of joy running down his cheek. He cuddled his newborn son until it was time to go to work.

Newcastle can be bitterly cold during the winter months, often blanketed in heavy snowfall. In previous years, people were snowed in. Some winters having over four feet of snow. Byker was a "community," and people pulled together if there was an emergency or neighbours needing help. So, when the snow blizzards arrived, people got out their shovels or whatever implement they had to hand and cleared the roads and paths.

Isabella did not get to use her new pram bought by her parents for several weeks until the snow had gone. She was simply happy to be in her house with the coal fire roaring and looking after BabyThomas. He was a contented baby with a huge appetite. He let everyone know when he was hungry with a very loud cry, which was like an alarm clock. Apart from letting Isabella know he was either hungry or had a dirty nappy that needed to be changed, he was a good baby.

Tommy could not wait to get home after he finished work to get to see his son and play with him while Isabella made the tea.

Both Tommy's and Isabella's parents would visit regularly tobsee Thomas, he was their first grandson, and they adored him.

Over the next couple of years, another son and a daughter were added to the Taylor family. A son called Alex, and a girl called Mary Ellen. Hopefully, that was their family complete now.

The house was becoming too small with three children There were only two bedrooms: one was Tommy's and Isabella's, which had a cot at the side for Mary Ellen, and the other bedroom was shared between Thomas Junior and Alex. Now it was ok, but Mary Ellen was now outgrowing her cot. They would need a bigger house soon.

Irene Richardson

Chapter Sixteen
Tommy's Plan

Tommy, who worked for one of the largest engineering factories in Newcastle, was now a Foreman in charge of 30 men on his floor. He never had a day off or was ever ill, and this was rewarded with a promotion to manager. A job that was a challenge as he was in charge now of two floors, Two Foremen and around 60 workers. Tommy thrived on a challenge and just loved his job, and of course, the big rise in his pay packet came in handy with three growing bairns.

Tommy never lost his temper; he was a gentle giant for want of a better description. He had the ability to see both sides of a situation and would try to resolve any problems without conflict. The management had obviously seen this over the years and had him earmarked for the position of Senior General Manager. The current manager, Fred Graham, was retiring due to ill health. Fred had worked there since he left school.

Tommy was summoned to the head office one day. His appointment with the "higher management" was to be at 3 o'clock.

A Newcastle Lass

All day, Tommy was trying to be calm. "What if I am getting paid off? What if they think I am not doing the job or not up to it?" He kept going over and over it on his way to the head office. Tommy told himself to calm down and just listen to what they have to say, stop worrying over something you are just surmising, "Cannot be that bad, get a grip man!"

Tommy was taken through to one of the offices that were used for management meetings. He was greeted by the receptionist, Milly, whom he knew "You will be fine Tommy. Stop your worrying and let us have one of your big smiles!" Milly said.

There were three men sitting behind a table in the room They asked him to take a seat and pointed to the chair in front of the table.

The man in the middle, Tommy immediately recognized as Mr. Ainsworth, the Head of Staff. However, the two men standing beside him were unfamiliar—though one of them struck a chord of recognition.

Mr. Ainsworth gestured toward them. "Tommy, this is Robert Wentworth and Charlie Anderson."

Before Tommy could respond, Charlie stepped forward and spoke first.

"Tommy Taylor, do you not recognize me? We went to Raby Street School together. I still remember how you sorted out a couple of big kids who were bullying me and nicking my dinner money every day."

"Oh man, Charlie Anderson, I remember you now. You moved away to Durham soon after; I always wondered how you were."

"Excuse me, gentlemen," said Mr. Ainsworth. "We have some business to discuss, and I'm sure you two can catch up over a pint later."

"Tommy, we have followed your time here at Reyrolles since you started as an apprentice and over the years have contributed all your skills within the company, not just your work but the managing your team of men on your floor, and we appreciate this and your loyalty to the Firm. With that said, we would like to offer you the position of Senior Head Manager, which is currently held by Fred Graham, who is retiring in three months. It will be a more challenging role being Senior Head Manager of all the workshops, but we believe that you are more than capable of this position. There will be of course, a considerable rise in your wages, and you would have to shadow Fred over the next three months. Have you any questions and would you like some time to think about it?"

Tommy was speechless for once in his life; the three men were waiting for his answer.

Tommy took a deep breath and said, "Thank you for considering me to take over Fred's position It will be very big shoes to fill, but I would welcome this generous offer and will do my best not to let you down."

Charlie piped up, "Tommy, we would not have chosen you if we did not think you were not capable of handling it…. Come on man, you deserve it!"

Mr. Ainsworth said, "We will get your new contract written and see to your wages today, and as from Monday, you will work alongside Fred. Thank you for coming in, and welcome to the management Tommy." All three men stood up and shook his hand.

Tommy left the office with a big grin on his face. As he passed Milly at the reception, she gave him a hug. "If anyone deserves this job, you do Tommy… well done! Now get away home and tell your Isabella."

Tommy burst through the front door, eager to tell Isabella the most amazing news ever. This would solve their problems; they could afford a bigger house now.

Isabella was cooking a pot of lamb stew for their tea.

Tommy grabbed her and swung her around and around.

"Be careful, ye daft bugger, I'll spill the stew!" spoke Isabella.

"Never mind the stew, pet come and sit yersel down, got some good news to tell you." Tommy was grinning from ear to ear.

"Ok," she sat down on his knee. Tommy kissed her, and she smelled of lamb stew.

"Got a big promotion to Senior Head Manager of the workshops, taking Fred Graham's place as he is retiring. Getting a big pay rise…. We can afford to move now; what do you say Issy?" Tommy always called her Issy.

Isabella was lost for words; all she could do was put her arms around him and give him a huge kiss.

After tea and the bairns were bathed and put to bed, Tommy and Isabella sat down to make some plans for their future.

Tommy started his new position the following week, shadowing Fred to learn the ins and outs of day-to-day management. Tommy was quick to learn and by the time Fred was ready to leave, Tommy was doing the job by himself.

New Job, New Challenge!

He was called to the Head Office for a meeting with Mr. Ainsworth on the Friday afternoon when Fred was due to leave. Fred was already seated in the office.

"Hello Tommy, please have a seat," said Mr. Ainsworth. "Just a quick run-through of your progress. Fred has given you a glowing report and has no doubt we have picked the right man for this job. So as from Monday, you will take over officially as Senior Head Manager. Fred has informed all the Heads of the Department, and they will in turn inform the workforce."

He turned to Fred. "Fred, we are at a loss as to what to say to you, but you are doing the right thing in stopping work and being with your loved ones during this sad time."

Fred had told them that he had been diagnosed with terminal cancer and wanted to spend what little few months he had left with his family.

"We want you to know that we are devastated that you are leaving but fully understand all the reasons why. We would like you to accept this gift from all who work here They have all contributed money and want you to use it as you wish. There is £900 in this wallet Fred; please accept this from the management, office staff and all your friends who work here. You have been an exemplary employee and a good friend to everyone. We will miss you."

Mr. Ainsworth had tears in his eyes as he shook Fred's hand and gave him the wallet of money. Fred could not say anything; he was so overwhelmed by the generosity and the kind words. Tommy hugged Fred and thanked him for all he had taught him over the last few weeks.

As Fred walked down the corridor, there were hundreds of workers gathered outside in the yard, clapping, and cheering for him. He did not expect that at all. My-my, what a day!

Mr. Ainsworth took Tommy aside and said, come back into the office. I need you to sign your new contract of employment.

Tommy looked at the contract with disbelief. He was to receive twice his current salary, which began on Monday. He signed the form, and Mr. Ainsworth countersigned it and asked Millie to officially witness it.

Tommy was on cloud nine walking home. Now Issy and him could make some real plans now. He felt like shouting at the top of his voice or doing cartwheels. He was so happy that he could give Issy and the bairns what they deserved, oh how he loved them.

By the time he reached home, it was getting dark and then bairns had been bathed and fed but were waiting to see their Dad and get a bedtime story from him. Tommy used to make up all sorts of stories and had them laughing and giggling, Issy used to tell him off as they would be wide awake and hyper, and it would take some time before they went off to sleep. But today was special, and he said that if they were good and went off to sleep quickly, next weekend, he would take them into town. He loved them dearly, and they were good bairns. They deserved to have a surprise, and now he had the money.

It had to be the toy department in Fenwicks, and they could choose something as a special treat! Of course, this sent their excitement through the roof. Issy had to give Tommy another playful telling-off, much to the delight of the bairns, who found it hilarious. Still giggling, they tried hard to go to sleep, thinking about a new toy!

Tommy and Isabella were sitting by the roaring coal fire. Tommy then told Isabella all that had happened today. Her eyes grew wide in disbelief. "Aww Tommy, I am so proud of you, not just what you have achieved at work but being the most humble, generous, loving

A Newcastle Lass

Husband and He kissed her and said, And I am proud of you too, my beautiful wife. Now let us go to bed; I am so worn out and tired with all the excitement of the day."

"Not too worn out and tired?" she asked with a cheeky grin on her face.

Irene Richardson

Chapter Seventeen
Moving House

Over the whole weekend, they were looking at houses to rent in the area, something with three or four bedrooms and a bit of a garden for the bairns to play in. There was one just a few streets away, but the landlord was asking too much.

Another one only had two bedrooms, but it had a garden, which was not right either. Just as they were about to give up, their next-door neighbor knocked on the door to tell them that there was a house three streets away that was not up for rent yet. Her brother had told her about it as he was looking for a bigger house, but it was just too big, and the rent was more than he could manage. They thanked her and took the details. They arranged to see it the following day, and the landlord met them outside the property.

It looked all right from outside, a small, neat garden at the front. They went through the front door into a spacious hall with stairs leading to the upstairs bedrooms. The living room looked nice and clean with a coal fire and a tiled fireplace surround, a space in one corner with a dining table and six chairs, and the Kitchen was spacious with a big larder, a good-sized gas cooker, a big stone sink for washing up with a hot water boiler above it. The main bedroom was large, and the other three were smaller but adequate for their needs. There was also a garden at the back, which was fenced, so perfect for the family.

Isabella loved it and smiled at Tommy, who was discussing the rent with the Landlord. They came to an agreement and the deal was done.

They could move in at the end of the month plus a month's rent in advance.

Tommy and Isabella were delighted with the house… exactly right, needs a lick of paint and some new wallpaper, but they knew that this was the one for them…. Now they had to start packing, etc. It was amazing how much stuff you keep but do not use! Nothing was thrown away. Someone would have use for these things. Clothes and shoes the bairns had grown out of went to some neighbours or were passed onto families that they knew would be grateful for them. Pots, pans, cooking utensils, cups, mugs, plates, bowls, bedding, old rugs, etc., that they had replaced with new ones and had not thrown out the old ones. Everything would be quite new to some needy families.

Moving day arrived, and they had been busy packing everything into boxes for easy transport to the house. Although it was only a few streets away, it took them all day to move everything. Parents and friends helped as much as they could, so by teatime, they had transported all their belongings and made up the beds for the bairns first so that they could go to sleep when it was their usual bedtime. Tommy and Isabella just slept in the living room for the night, they would sort their bedroom out tomorrow.

It had been a full-on day, and they were exhausted. Sitting on the rug in front of the fire, Tommy put his arms around Isabella and said, "Well Bonny lass we did it. It will all be worth it. Are you happy Issy?" She turned and kissed him.

"I am more than happy, and I think we are having another bairn too; how do you feel about that?" Tommy was over the moon; he had always wanted a big family, a house full of little ones.

"You know what, Issy? I must be the happiest and luckiest man alive!"

The house underwent a transformation over the next few months. All the rooms were either painted or wallpapered. New rugs on the floor with new Lino underneath. The place looked fresh and clean.

Isabella was now 4 months pregnant and was starting to show she was keeping well but had dreadful back pain. She put it down to all the moving and decorating. She would take it easier now and try to take more rest. She was looking forward to a new baby in the house. She had kept some baby clothes from the boys and Mary Ellen. Now that they were all settled in, she would be able to sit at the fire and do some knitting. She could only knit with limited colors of wool, no pinks, or blues. So, it was white, lemon, pale green, and beige balls of wool she bought for her knitting basket, which sat at the side of her armchair. She had a few new patterns too, that would suit either a boy or a girl.

The bairns settled into their new home very quickly. Alex and Tommy shared a bedroom, and Mary Ellen had the small bedroom. The biggest room was Tommy and Isabella's, and they kept the other small room as a spare whenever the parents came to babysit and stay over.

Isabella had just loved picking the colors of paint and wallpaper for each room. Tommy had a mate Stan who was a painter and decorator, and he did all the work for them as Tommy was working flat out in his new position at work.

Young Tommy and Alex were mostly next door; the couple there, William, and Elsie, had two young boys, James and John, who were about a year older than

Tommy and Alex but just loved playing with them. Elsie did not mind one bit as it kept her boys out of her hair, and she could get on with her dressmaking. She was an exceptionally talented dressmaker, and everyone around used to get Elsie to make their clothes. She charged very reasonable prices too.

Isabella needed some new clothes, and so did growing Mary Ellen, so she asked Elsie to make a few things for her.

Isabella went into Newcastle to buy some material etc. Elsie had given her a note of what to buy. Isabella would choose the colors, paper pattern buttons and zips that were required.

Elsie had every color of thread, so this was not needed.

She had seen some lovely blue cotton with sprigs of white and lemon blossom for a summer dress; she loved blue. There was also a pale green and cream with a narrow strip of green that was also very pretty for Summer, so she bought that too. After checking out the amount needed from the back of a maternity pattern, she had chosen which would do for the two dresses. The dresses would also need some lace trimming for the collar. Isabella bought some in white and some in cream. Now for Mary Ellen's dresses, she needed two for the summer as well. Pale Pink and lemon cotton was chosen for her. The pink material had little rosebuds, and the lemon had white rosebuds with tiny green leaves. Mary was delighted with her purchases. It had been a while since she had this kind of money to spend. Usually, a trip to the second-hand shop would keep them all in clothes and shoes. The children grew fast these days and when Tommy Junior grew out of his clothes, then Alex got them.

Mary Ellen had some clothes given to her by a cousin of Tommy's who had three girls in their family.

As Isabella walked home with her new purchases, she felt happy and content not to be watching the pennies these days. They were not rich, but with Tommy's salary being doubled, they were now comfortable.

Elsie got to work on Isabella's and Mary Ellen's dresses and were ready in two weeks. They were beautiful. Isabella used to like sewing at school but had not had the time to make anything these days apart from darning holes in socks, patches on elbows, taking down dress hems and lengthening trousers for the boys.

Isabella was now 6 months pregnant; one morning, when she was clearing the breakfast dishes, she felt a low-down pain, which took her breath away, just wind cramps, she told herself, but they came again stronger. It was at this time that Isabella's Mam and Dad arrived. They had promised to take Isabella and the bairns to the Fair at the Town Moor to the Fun-fair. This was an annual

event where the Travelling Community came with lorries and trailers loaded with amusements and rides, side shows, stalls, etc.

There were also vans that sold hot dogs and saveloy dips, a fish and chip van too; these did a roaring trade. Everyone was hungry as the air was filled with their tempting smell.

A week that Geordie Folk attended to in their thousands. Everyone had a fun time.

When Grace entered the front door, she heard Isabella scream. She rushed through to the kitchen where Isabella was holding her stomach and was bleeding down below; quick, get Isabella into the car and get her to the Infirmary as fast as you can, God forbid she is losing the baby.

Isabella lost her baby; it was a girl; she did not survive at only 6 months.

Isabella and Tommy were in shock; this was not meant to be, and Isabella's health was now more important as they had been advised that Isabella should not have any more babies. Her womb needed to be removed, but that would be when she had recovered from this miscarriage.

Tommy held her on the settee in front of the fire when they got home. Harry and Grace had now left, the bairns were in bed, and the house was quiet.

Tommy was the first to speak. "I know you wanted this baby Issy, but it is God's way of telling you this little girl was not ready for this world yet and that your health would have suffered a great deal too. We should enjoy and be thankful for the healthy family we have, my love." Isabella snuggled into his chest and felt the concern, warmth and love he had for her and their family.

He was a good man with a heart of gold, and although she had lost her baby, she knew she would not forget her, and her wonderful husband would support her during this awful time.

Isabella was more upset about the loss of her baby girl than she thought she would be. She cried at the least little thing sometimes snapped at the bairns or Tommy for no reason at all. Felt miserable a lot of the time. Isabella tried to shake this melancholy off, but what she did not realize was that this was her hormones playing havoc with her feelings.

Tommy tried his hardest to cheer her up; he had never known Isabella to be this way. She was always laughing, busying around, giving hugs to the family and affection to Tommy. He missed the old Issy.

Tommy had had an accident whilst putting up a bookshelf in the Bairns bedroom. They loved reading but there was nowhere to put the many amounts of books, so they were all over the place. Just as he was hammering the last nail in a bracket, he looked away for a second and hammered the nail through his finger. He went to his doctor to get it seen, and while he was there, he mentioned Isabella's mood swings, anxiety, panic attacks also a lack of enthusiasm, just not like Isabella at all. Dr Jamison, who knew Tommy and his family well, gave him a prescription for some iron pills for her and told him all this would pass soon as her hormones got back to normal. Isabella was a strong woman and needed time to grieve. A few trips out to the coast could help; try it and see. A bit of fresh air is a tonic for everyone.

Irene Richardson

Chapter Eighteen
Tynemouth Sands

Tommy heeded the Doctor's advice about Isabella and tried to take Isabella and the family out a little bit more. It did work, and Isabella, within a month or so, was more like a normal self.

The Summer that year was extremely hot, and the family were planning a trip to the seaside. Tynemouth Sands. While Tommy got the excited bairns dressed, Isabella made up a picnic hamper to take with them. She made egg sandwiches, sausage rolls, iced fairy cakes, a flask of tea for her and Tommy, some juice for the bairns, buckets and spades and a beach ball.

They now had a second-hand car, an old banger, but it worked and did the job. They packed the car and set off. It was a gorgeous sunny day, and everyone was excited.

When they got there and picked a spot on the beach, the blanket spread out, and buckets, spaces etc., put to one side. Tommy, Alex, and Mary Ellen got into their swimming costumes a drink of juice, and then they were away to the edge of the sea, which was safe and shallow. Tommy and Isabella were near and could keep an eye on them building a sandcastle. After about an hour, Tommy went to fetch the bairns for something to eat and drink. They were all having a fun time. They were playing with some new friends, two boys, building a sort of castle with a moat around it, which they were trying in vain to fill with buckets of seawater. It kept sinking into the sand, but they went back and forth to the sea to get more water as bairns do.

They asked Isabella if their two new friends could have something to eat as well, as they were hungry, and their Mam had only brought a packet of crisps.

Isabella went over to the woman and asked if it was ok for her bairns to have something to eat with them and she was more than welcome to join them as they had enough food to feed the whole of Tynemouth Beach. The woman laughed and said that was kind. They introduced themselves; her name was Joan Winship, and her twin boys were Sean and Michael.

After they had their sandwiches, cakes, and tea, Tommy took all the bairns back to their sandcastle to help rebuild it, the tide had come in and had washed most of it away.

Isabella and Joan sat on the blanket and laughed at Tommy, trying to fill the moat.

They got on well. Joan and her boys were in lodgings in Byker. "What a coincidence, I know Byker very well," said Isabella, "and we now live in Walker, not too far away. You must come and have a cup of tea and a natter."

"Thank you, you are kind, that would be very nice," replied Joan.

During their conversations, it turned out that Joan was being evicted from her lodgings for rent arrears, her husband had gone off with another woman to London, and she was left with the twins. She was looking for a live-in housekeeper job, but some employers did not want children.

"Joan, I have an idea; let me speak to Tommy. I need some help with the house, and we have one spare bedroom, and I am sure our boys do not mind sharing a room together, so that your boys could have one of the bedrooms for themselves. What do you think? Mind you I will have to run it by Tommy, but I think he will be ok with it as he is always saying I could do with some help around the house," Isabella spoke to Tommy, who thought it was an excellent idea, but Joan will have to have a trial period to see if it was going to work out ok?

Joan was over the moon when Isabella told her what Tommy had said, "You are a life saver. I thought we would be out on the streets, and I promise you I will not let you down."

Joan, the twins, and a few worldly belongings moved into Tommy and Isabella's house the following week. She was in awe of this beautiful house and looked forward to keeping it shining and clean for them.

The twins had had a good talking to by their Mam on behaving while they lived there. She had been given a chance of a new life here, a roof over her head and no worries about finding the rent money. She was lucky to have a narrow escape from the landlord as he was hinting at paying her arrears in kind, and she knew what that meant.

Isabella was an angel sent by God, she thought when everything seemed hopeless. It would mean being on the streets or the workhouse for her, and what would happen to her boys, they would be taken off her. Must not think of that!

This was her only chance of making a fresh start and Joan would work every hour to make this happen. Isabella and Tommy were such a lovely, genuine couple whom she would not let down.

They soon settled into the family's way of life, and everyone seemed to get on well. Joan loved keeping the house spick and span, did all the washing and ironing, and did the shopping as well.

Isabella could not believe how lucky she was meeting Joan a few months ago on Tynemouth Beach. She was a godsend, and marvelled at the way ran the household, so well and organized too. Her twins were lovely boys and got on so well with their classmates.

Irene Richardson

Chapter Nineteen
Productivity

Tommy was enjoying his new position as Senior Head Manager. He was a fair man with the workforce and could be relied upon to meet the completion and deadline of orders. New contracts were coming in daily, and he had to organize overtime for workers.

Tommy had an idea and needed to run it past the Board of Directors. He met them in the Board Room to hear his plan to step up production. Those present were Mr. Swanston. Mr Ross, Mr Davison, and Mr Swanston's secretary, Mrs Campbell, took the notes of the Meeting.

Tommy was the first to speak. "Thank you for taking the time to meet with me, gentlemen. I would like to discuss a plan I have to increase productivity, complete orders, and deliveries on time, and keep our workmen in full-time employment with an opportunity for more overtime, which means more money in their pocket."

"Sounds like you have been busy Tommy. Let us hear what you have to say."

He outlined his plans for higher productivity, which was to set up a time and rate for the individual engineering parts that were made on the shop floors, simply by allowing time for setting up the machine and collecting materials needed. Then the part to be produced would be timed on how long it would take to complete, then calculated how many could be made each hour. This target would be recorded on the operative's job card, and on completion, the supervisor would check the productivity and timing, and the operator would be paid a small bonus depending on quantity and, of course, quality.

Productivity would be higher, plus having a happier workforce with an incentive to make more money. It would be an opportunity for some men to earn more as some were struggling to earn a decent living. So, it is a win-win situation for both sides. Each engineering shop would need a full-time, experienced man to do the Timing, etc. Each shop floor had several experienced older men who would welcome the chance of a new position and challenge like this.

That all sounds like a good plan; you have certainly done your homework. Do you have your ideas written down? Tommy said "yes, I have them here. I took the liberty of asking Milly to type up the details" Tommy handed them over to Mr Brown who read Tommy's proposals.

"You have certainly covered every aspect of a higher production thoroughly and judging from your report, I can see this working. So,

Tommy, we will give you a free hand to get the ball rolling. Well, done Tommy; we appreciate all your hard work. Well, done! Now let us see if Mrs Campbell here can rustle up some tea, eh?"

Tommy was on a high walking home. "Can't wait to tell Issy all that has happened today."

Issy was making Poached haddock for tea; he could smell it as he opened the front door. He swung her off her feet, fish slice in hands; she said, "You are one happy man tonight, Tommy… is it because you are having poached haddock?" she chided, and he laughed.

"I will give you poached haddock wifey! Your clever clog of a husband has just had his productivity ideas accepted."

Isabella put down the fish slice and gave Tommy a big hug. "You, my wonderful husband, you are the cleverest man I know, and did I ever tell you the best kisser too?" Tommy laughed and gave his wife a big kiss to prove it.

"Right now, Missus, your clever husband needs feeding. Where is that poached haddock? I am starving."

They had their dinner, and Isabella had made a Treacle Tart and custard for afterwards. They sat contented by the fire after they had finished eating, comfortable in the silence and each other's company. The house was quiet; everyone had gone to bed early, so it was just the two of them.

Tommy had fallen asleep, and Isabella looked over at him, sleeping peacefully with a smile on his face. She thought how lucky she was to have such a kindhearted husband who put his wife and family first. Oh, how she adored this man! She whispered to him, "I love you, Tommy Taylor."

Tommy opened one eye and said, "Get yourself into the bedroom Issy, and I will show you how much I love you!"

Irene Richardson

Chapter Twenty
Contentment

Isabella and Joan were sitting by the fire with a mug of tea, having a break from a huge washing they had done. All pegged out on the clothesline, it was blowing in the gentle breeze and drying well. All the boys were at school, and Mary Ellen was in the rear garden with the girl next door, playing with their dolls. The back door was open, and Isabella could hear them chattering as they had some milk and custard cream biscuits.

Joan had baked yesterday afternoon, and they were having a slice of delicious Madeira Cake with their tea. All was going well. Isabella loved having Joan and her boys living with them. She was an absolute godsend and could not imagine the house without them.

Tommy's plan for more productivity gave the men an opportunity to earn extra money. A few men put their names forward for the position of supervisor and were duly interviewed.

Four Men were successful and were due to start soon. Tommy was to concentrate on putting his suggested plan into action for a trial run on the smallest of the workshops, which had 20 machines.

First, a small wooden office was built at one end of the factory for the supervisor, who was equipped with his stopwatch, a clipboard, and a pen to decide and time of a particular part to be made.

After sourcing the materials needed and the timing of setting up the machine, he recorded the amount of time it took to make and finish it off. Tommy then had to add in break/ toilet times etc. A final run-through plus multiplying the number needed for the order.

A Job Card was made and put into a docket holder on the office wall of all the current jobs. This Job Card was a record of the work to be carried out. The card was inserted into a timing device on the wall, which stamped the starting time, and when the work was completed, the job card card marked with the finish time.

They were checked and sent to the Head Office so they could process the delivery to the client. The cards were then passed onto the Wages Office. for assessment of the extra money earned by the Employee if completion was faster than the original time quoted to finish the job. This would be added to his wage.

Tommy had a goal to have all the men on this new timing of jobs, and they in return, could see the monetary benefits. It was a challenging time, and every extra in their pay packet by working overtime would be more than welcome. It gave the men a bit of hope that they could have extra money in their weekly wage packet. Once the set up was complete, there was an exciting buzz in all the workshops. The men knew that they had to work hard for the benefits that the company had made available to them. And they did!

Production was up by 25% during the first couple of weeks of implementing the "Timing Job Cards."

The workers' wage packets showed quite a bit of extra money in them at the end of the first week.

The second week showed a further rise in production and showed in the men's Wage Packets.

Everyone was up on a high, no one more than Tommy to see his plan working and getting results. He was anxious at first that it would work and if the men would be on board. But he need not have had any doubts, and this was confirmed when Tommy was summoned to Mr Atkinson's office after the first month of setting up his ideas.

"Tommy, come in, lad and have a seat," Mr Atkinson pointed to a chair. "Well Tommy, as you know, the Board of Directors gave you a free rein to set up your Time and Productivity idea last month and have been watching your progress. The men have embraced this new way of working and they can see the positive results in their wage packets each week.

We, the Management, are delighted at the amount of time and effort you have put into this Tommy, and with that said, "We are increasing your wages another £10 per week as of this weekend. You are an asset to this company, and we are pleased to have you working for us, well done lad!"

Tommy was speechless as he shook Mr Atkinson's hand and went back to his office, "Oh do I need a mug of strong tea now?" he chuckled to himself. "Wait till I tell Issy; she'll know exactly how to spend the extra cash." He chuckled to himself... he adored Issy, and he would give her anything she wanted, well if he could afford it!

They had always talked about having a week's holiday in Blackpool in the Summer, going there by coach. Well, this extra money every week would more than be enough for their holiday and they could take Joan and the twins Sean and Michael with them. Tommy loved the twins they were so funny and got on great with his offspring. They had become one extra big family. Let us see what Issy has to say.

When Tommy got home, it was dark, raining, and cold. He headed straight for the roaring coal fire in the Living room, sat in his armchair, and warmed his frozen feet in front of the fire. There was just enough room for him as the bairns were all seated on the floor together, getting warm.

There was a lovely smell coming from the kitchen where Issy and Joan were cooking, "What is for tea Issy?"

Mary Ellen answered, "It's sossis casroll," and they all laughed.

Michael piped up, "Sausage casserole, and Mam has made an apple pie as well."

They all tucked into the "sossis casroll" and the hot apple pie, now with full bellies, they all sat around the fire contented. Tommy, Isabella, and Joan had the armchairs, and the bairns sat on the floor.

Tommy was the first to speak. He told them about going to Mr Atkinson's office and how his plans had gone and how pleased the Management were about the success of it and the best bit of it was the £10 rise. They were cheering, and Mary Ellen joined in as well, although she did not know why or what for. Everyone laughed.

"Right, you lot, time for bed! Come on, I will tuck you all in and read you a story," said Joan. Off they all went, giving Tommy and Isabella a kiss and a "night night" Tommy always finished with" and watch the bugs do not bite." Off they went with Joan, everyone wanting a different story.

When they were alone, Tommy mentioned the idea of all of them going to Blackpool for a week in the Summer as he now could afford a holiday for them and how did she feel about taking Joan and the twins too? Isabella jumped up and kissed Tommy several times." Hey Bonnie lass, steady now, so I take that to be, yes?"

Isabella said that Joan has been a godsend to her. She was like a sister, and Sean and Michael were like brothers to their bairns, so yes, she would love to give them a holiday too.

Chapter Twenty-One
Family Outings

Tommy and Isabella talked about their holiday to Blackpool for hours, and Isabella said she would go into Newcastle tomorrow to the Bus Station Office at the Haymarket to make enquiries. Also pick up a newspaper with bed and breakfast ads for accommodation in Blackpool.

As usual, Tommy was away at work at 5.30. A 30-minute walk, so he was there by 6 a.m. He always arrived a bit early to check the progress of the jobs from the day before and to make sure the completed job cards were ready to send off to the head office so that they could be processed. The orders that were still to be carried out were arranged in date order so that the men could be working straight away on them. Any new contracts would be handed into his office would be written on job cards, put in order in the wall dockets and ready for the workers to start when they arrived at 7.

A mug of tea was handed to him by Mabel, who ran the canteen. It was a sort of ritual each morning. Sometimes there was a hot scone and butter. Mabel was a lovely woman who had worked in the canteen since leaving school and now ran it like clockwork. Her work was her life. Her husband had died years ago, and with no family, her job was her reason to get up in the morning, she loved it. Tommy and Mabel got on like a house on fire.

They chatted and joked with each other whilst Tommy had his tea and scone. Sometimes Mabel would bring a mug for herself to drink. Tea was finished, and then it was back to business. Always a busy day ahead for them both.

Isabella sat at the table that morning with Joan and the bairns having breakfast. She could not wait to tell Joan about the surprise holiday to Blackpool.

There was porridge for breakfast. Warmed everyone up for going out in the freezing weather. It was very cold and frosty this morning Everyone was wrapped up in jumpers, warm coats, hats, scarves, and mittens to go to school. Mary Ellen was to go to the nursery just around the corner; she just loved it. She had friends to play with, had lots of coloring in, and even had milk and a biscuit for everyone. She was there for a half day, but sometimes when Isabella had to go into town, the nursery teacher, Mrs.Dunnett, would let her stay until teatime. Mary Ellen loved Mrs Dunnett… not as much as her Mam and Joan, but quite a lot.

Whenever she was allowed to stay for the afternoon she had her lunch there as well. She liked that. That was the case today as Isabella had planned to go into Newcastle to find bus times and train times for their Blackpool holiday. She was just so excited to tell Joan.

All the bairns were away at school and Mary Ellen was at the nursery, so she was free until 3 o'clock.

Joan finished clearing up the dishes. Time for her and Isabella to have a cup of tea in peace in front of the roaring fire.

Once they were settled, Isabella said, "Joan, I have something to ask you... Tommy and I were talking last night about a week's trip away on holiday."

Joan interrupted and said, "You know I will look after the house when you're away, and if you want to go yourselves, I will look after the bairns too, you know I will."

"Joan, shut up a minute, will you? We want to ask if you, Michael, and Sean would like to come as well as a huge thank you from us for all the work you do for us. You know we think of you as family!"

Joan's mouth was wide open in disbelief at what Isabella had just said, "Joan, shut your mouth; you will catch flies!"

Tears were now rolling down Joan's cheeks, "So that's a YES, is it?" Joan could not speak, so she nodded her head in between sobs.

When Joan stopped crying, she said, "Isabella, thank you so much. I have never had a holiday in my life and never thought I would. You and Tommy have given me and the boys a lifeline when I thought it would be the streets or the workhouse. I am forever grateful to you both for that, but this is just the most amazing thing anyone has done for us. Thank you, thank you," and started to cry again.

They made plans to go into Newcastle today to find out about buses trains, etc.

Both women were so excited, grinning from ear to ear as they walked into town.

Anyone passing must have thought they were not the full shilling as they were acting like silly schoolgirls!

Grace made enquiries at the Haymarket Bus Station, and the man behind the desk wrote all the information down: cost of return tickets for adults and children, dates, bus times, journey time, the stops at Hexham, Carlisle, and Morecambe, and then arriving at Blackpool. He also wrote the names of a couple of guest houses to s

Isabella and Joan came away feeling elated; it all seemed so now. They decided that after checking out the train, which was quicker but much dearer if they took the bus, they would have more money to spend while they were there.

"Just to talk it over with Tommy when he gets home tonight and obviously the bairns too" said Isabella.

"We will have trouble getting them off to sleep tonight! Just as well it is Saturday tomorrow, and no school."

Joan thought it may not just be the bairns that would not sleep with excitement, but her too.

Beef Mince Pie topped with a flaky pastry lid, gravy, mashed potatoes, and peas and carrots, followed by a creamy rice pudding.

Everything was about ready when Tommy came whistling through the front door. The table was set for their tea. Everyone tucked in; it was freezing outside, but there was a huge coal fire burning in the fireplace. The room was cosy and warm, and everyone with a full belly too. Sheer Contentment!!

Isabella told Tommy about her day in Newcastle: how she had gotten all the information about the bus to Blackpool and how helpful the man at the bus station had been. She showed Tommy the bus times and ticket prices, saying that those under 5 years old are free. Then she told him of the two Boarding Houses recommended by the man, too. Joan was eavesdropping whilst washing the dishes in the kitchen to see what Tommy's reply was. She could not wait to hear what he thought. "Issy, that is great and less than I thought, we will me thinks we will all gan on our holidays, what do you say pet? Isabella hugged and kissed him, the bairns had seen this and were giggling.

"Right, you lot," said Tommy, "gather round, I have something to tell you." All the children's faces were all smiles but also wondered what he was going to say. "How would you all like to go on a bus trip to Blackpool for a week's holiday in August?" The young ones had not heard of Blackpool, so Tommy told them it was a big seaside town with lots of things to do donkey rides on the beach, fun fairs, a circus, and other shows and staying in a boarding house. Fish and Chips, ice cream, candy floss, penny arcade machines. Of course, he must explain a lot of these activities as they had no idea. They had lots and lots of questions for Tommy, all of which he explained in a language they understood, and he was just so patient with them all. Everyone was excited, and it was almost 10 o'clock before the last sleepy eyes closed, dreaming of Blackpool.

It was Saturday. Next morning, no work, no school, just family time together. It was a cold April day but dry. They decided to go to Jesmond Dene for the day, a lovely park with summerhouses, streams, ducks and even a small boat pond to sail the wooden boats that Tommy had made for them all. They took their fishing nets and buckets to catch some tadpoles in the river, which ran through the Dene. Isabella and Joan made sandwiches and packed slices of Joan's home-made cake, and off they went for the day.

They all had a fun-packed day and were very tired by the time they reached home. Had a quick tea of bacon, sausage, and fried egg with a slice of fried bread and a mug of tea. Then off to bed for the bairns, too late for a bath. They were fast asleep in minutes with a smile in their faces.

The adults sat around the fire, comfortable with each other in silence.

Chapter Twenty-Two
Millie

Tommy's car was not big enough to fit everyone in and was not used much these days. Mostly stood at the front door in the street. Seemed a waste of money not being used. Tommy walked to work. Isabella walked to the nursery, school and into Newcastle or got the bus. The weather was bad, and the bus stop was only 100 yards away.

The same for Joan, she walked to the shops, etc.

Tommy thought it was about time to sell it.

That night, when Tommy got home and had his tea and was sitting at the fire in his armchair with Isabella, she was sewing something… there was always something to be mended these days with a growing family.

"Issy, what do you think about getting a large van and fitting the back out with seats so that we can use it for our outings? Would be much handier to fit everyone in; I can fit benches in the back and rugs on the floor. Plenty of room for everyone." She thought it was an amazing idea, and they could just pack the van and go off whenever or wherever they wanted.

And so, within a few weeks, Tommy had a smart Dark Blue Van of which he was quite proud of. With the help of Isabella's brother, who had been a joiner to trade along with another mate Jim, they soon have the van looking great. Isabella and Joan had been shopping and had bought a Primus stove, a kettle, a couple of pans, a few bits of second-hand cutlery, mugs, etc., enough to make a meal or snack for them all. Alex had built the benches with lids and hinges so that they would double up as storage for cooking equipment, blankets, and tins of foodstuff. Another bench held large containers that could be filled with water for drinking and washing, towels and facecloths. Not forgetting the soap, washing up liquid and cleaning stuff, in fact everything that was needed for a day out or even an overnight stop if they were sleeping over. Also, some cushions for the benches were made of the same material, so no sore bums during a journey! They decided to call the van Millie

The following Sunday, they decided to have a trip to Seahouses on the north coast for the day. Tommy, Isabella, and Joan were up at dawn while the family was sleeping to load the van with food, drinks, towels, bathing costumes, buckets, and spades. They needed a clean change of clothing (just in case of an accident) and things that they did not need. Van was all packed and ready to go; Joan woke the bairns to get up for breakfast. There were a lot of protests and groans like, "But it's still dark; I'm tired, etc."

Tommy went through to the bedroom and said, "Last one up is being left behind. 'Cos the rest of us are going to Seahouses in the van for the day!"

A Newcastle Lass

There were squeals of delight, and they raced through for their breakfast which was eaten in record time, washed and ready, with buckets and spades in their hands. They all stood waiting… in mismatched clothes, and no one had combed their hair in the excitement.

Tommy, Isabella, and Joan had a laughing fit! Joan sorted them all out, and they were ready to go.

The trip to Seahouses took a little while, but the van was a bit older and slower so they got there safely. It was still early, and some of the bairns were still tired, but they fell asleep and were almost asleep as soon as they set off. They had a fabulous, fun day out. They ran about all day and were quite worn out when it was time to set off back home.

The sun had shone all day for them with just a slight breeze, perfect for a family day out.

When they got home and unpacked, Tommy locked up the van and said, "Thank you Millie, you have done us proud today."

The family had many more trips on the weekends, and Millie, bless her, got them to wherever they decided to go safely. Joan kept thinking what Tommy had said about being a family; she was so touched. What a lovely thing to say. She felt privileged to be included in trips such as today, and her twins had never really experienced such generosity, kindness, and love.

Irene Richardson

Chapter Twenty-Three
Mystery Trip

The next excursion was to be a "Mystery Trip." When they told all the bairns that there was to be a Mystery Trip on Sunday, they were all extremely excited. They were asking questions like where, how, and even what a Mystery Trip is.

Tommy said, "Well if I told you, it would not be a mystery, would it.

We could call it a Surprise Trip if you like; you all like surprises, don't you?"

So, it was unanimous that it was to be a surprise trip!

What everyone did not know was that Tommy had organized an amazing surprise for them all!

Once everyone was in bed and asleep, Tommy, Isabella, and Joan sat by the fire and discussed where this surprise trip would be. "We can't go too far in Millie as she is getting older, so within about an hour's drive will be ok," said Tommy.

Isabell and Joan suggested places to go, but Tommy always had an excuse for the suggestions such as "too far, been there, not enough to do for the bairns," etc.

"North Shields," said Tommy, "not been there, and there are lots of fishing boats at the harbour, and we all could have fish and chips at the café. How does that sound?"

So, it was agreed. But secretly, Tommy had something planned.

Sunday came, and everyone was up early. They packed Millie with everything they needed.

It was a lovely day; the sun was shining; everyone was in the van and off they went.

The bairns just loved the harbour, lots of fishing boats tied up in all assorted colours, and each one had its name on the side. Names like Geordie Lass, Tyne Rover, Bertha Belle, Northern Star and so on. After an hour of exploring, everyone was feeling quite hungry, so it was time to have their fish and chips at the café.

The waitress pushed several tables together to seat the family all together. Fish and chips were ordered for everyone, tea for Tommy, Isabella, and Joan, and the bairns had orange squash the waiter set the table with cutlery and brought bottles of tomato and brown sauce, malt vinegar, salt, and pepper and several plates of bread and butter.

Everyone was hungry; the fresh air on the coast gave them all an appetite. Fish, chips, bread and butter, tea and juice were eaten, and there was not a crumb left. Tommy loaded everyone back in Millie.

Tommy drove a couple of miles out into the surrounding countryside and pulled up at a farm. Everyone wondered why.

Tommy got everyone out. "Just one more surprise, well two surprises actually."

They all went into a nearby barn, and there was a female dog with six puppies who were 12 weeks old.

They were a cross between a Shepherd dog and a black Labrador, so some were black, and some were black with white patches.

The bairns just loved the puppies and were ever so excited. "Can we have one please, please?"

Tommy replied, "No, you can't have one." They all looked sad and dejected. Then he added, "You can have two!" Everyone was jumping around, including Isabella and Joan.

Then they all decided on which two to take home. Now that was what you would call a Mystery with an amazing surprise.

Dogs and family all loaded into Millie, and they set off for home. During the drive home, they picked out names for the dogs. They were males.

A Newcastle Lass

Suggestions such as Thunder, Robbie, Rover, Sammy, Nero, Bennie, Kenny and many more. After much deliberation, they chose Robbie and Rover.

Isabella hugged Tommy when they got home, he had secretively bought baskets and bedding, bowls, collars, leads, dog food, food and water bowls and anything else he thought they would need.

"Tommy, you are the most loving and generous man in the whole of Newcastle, and I love you to bits. Thank you for today."

Over the next few weeks, the dogs settled in with the family. Robbie and Rover just adored the bairns, and they adored them back.

It was near the time to go to Blackpool, their long-awaited trip.

Now that they had the dogs, what would happen to them? Tommy asked a couple of friends if they would look after them for a week, but they could not do so for one reason or another. Then just when he thought that he would have to cancel the trips, their next-door neighbor Frances offered to look after them by letting them stay in their own home, the back door would be open during the day so that the dogs could go out into the garden. They could be sleeping in their own beds at night and be more settled than in a stranger's house. Tommy thought this was an excellent idea and said he would get all their food and biscuits organized and gave Frances £20 for this! She refused to take the money, but with much persistence on Tommy's side, she eventually agreed to take his money.

Irene Richardson

Chapter Twenty-Four
Blackpool calling

Their trip to Blackpool had arrived; it was now the beginning of August.

Cases packed, and off they went to catch the bus at the Haymarket Bus Station. Isabella's brother had driven them there in Millie loaded with suitcases, and everyone was excited.

It would be a long journey, but Joan had packed colouring books and crayons, snap cards and some sweets and juice to keep them occupied. The bus would also be making a few stops on the way, so that would be good to stretch their legs and the bairns to have a little run about near where the bus was to be parked, usually beside the Public Toilets.

The bus driver's name was Willy, and as the bairns got on the bus, he said to them with a smile on his face, "Now you lot look like trouble, will have to keep an eye out for you, mind you I am easily bribed with one of those sweeties you have!"

"We will be good Mr. Willy, we promise, and Mary Ellen will give you one of her sweeties," said Michael. They all fell about

A Newcastle Lass

laughing, especially Willy. The only one not laughing was Mary Ellen.

Passengers and their cases were on the bus; it was full, and everyone was excited about going on their holidays. "Everyone all comfortable?" asked Willy. "Well then off we go!" Everyone cheered, and the bus pulled out of Haymarket Bus Station on its way to Blackpool. The first stop was Hexham. There was not much to see, but it was a chance to stretch the legs and use the toilet. As usual, there was a queue at the Ladies, so Tommy went with the boys to the ice-cream cart that was parked nearby. Obviously, it was a good trade with the buses stopping and 40 passengers per bus for an ice-cream cone in this weather.

By the time they were served, the women and Mary Ellen were back.

Everyone had a cone with one scoop of vanilla ice-cream, which they had to eat quickly before it was time for the bus to start in the next part of the journey.

Back on the bus and ready to go again, Willy shouted, "Did no-one buy me an ice cream. What a stingy lot you are." On hearing that, little Mary Ellen, who was at the front of the bus with Isabella, gives Willy one of her sweeties. "Thank you, pet." She went back to her seat with a smile on her face.

Off the bus went with Willy sucking his sweetie. Someone in the back started a singsong. The old songs were the best! Ten Green Bottles was a poular one.

The bairns were being incredibly good on the journey.

The other passengers took a shine to them and played games with them; they loved the attention. They were the only youngsters on the bus, apart from a teenage brother and sister and a teenage couple who were courting and kept smooching in the back of the bus. Mary Ellen was fascinated and stood in front of them, staring. The couple shooed her away and gave her some of their chocolate. That did the trick. Mary Ellen went back to her seat and ate her square of chocolate and promptly went back to the couple to hopefully get some more chocolate. They gave her another square and said it was all finished now. Mary Ellen ran back to her seat and scoffed down the chocolate.

Within five minutes, she was feeling sick. Joan, who was sitting beside her, noticed her change of colour and promptly pulled out a brown paper bag for her to be sick in. Tummy emptied; Mary Ellen felt a bit better. Joan suggested she should take a nap, and MaryEllen cuddled into her and fell asleep at once. No-one knew that Mary Ellen had also eaten all her own bag of sweeties as well!

The next stop was Carlisle; again, a stop at the public toilets. There was also a van that sold cups of tea and sandwiches. There was a long queue, and Isabella was standing about midway in the queue. She was hoping there would be something left. It was okay. The man who owned the van was a regular at the car park and had made enough sandwiches and pies to feed the whole of Carlisle. Isabella bought a choice of sandwiches, pies, and some rock cakes for everyone. Three mugs of tea and bottles of orange squash.

Once passengers had been to the toilet and bought from the Van Man Sydney, who Willie knew as this was his regular bus journey. They were all head counted and ready to go again to the next stop, which was Morecambe, another popular holiday town. Willie sometimes had passengers who were going to Morecambe for their holidays and got off there.

The journey passed quickly and quietly Most of the passengers were asleep, and the bus was quiet apart from the odd snorer. The bairns got a fit of the giggles and tried to copy the snoring noise.

Morecambe came into view, and the passengers who were getting off the bus there were busy gathering any rubbish they had ready to put in the bin in the car park whilst straightening their Clothes and giving a quick brush of their hair. Usually, everyone had a "flathead" after travelling for a good few hours.

The bus was parked in the car park, along with a few other trip buses. Everyone needing the toilet had to be back on the bus in 15 minutes as this was a short stopover.

The next part of the journey passed quickly; everyone was getting excited as they were getting nearer.

Irene Richardson

The passengers started to gather their belongings together, anxious to not forget anything. The mood was getting lighter, and everyone was smiling, "This is it, we are here, yippee!"

No one was more excited than the bairns They were jumping up and down when they got off the bus and parents were finding their cases. Mary Ellen saw the boys jumping up and down She did not know why but joined them in jumping… she liked jumping!

The boarding house that was recommended to Isabella by the man at the Information and Ticket Office in Newcastle.

He said, "There was a lovely Boarding House within walking distance of the Bus Park." The Carville Guest House owned by a lady called Mrs. Liz Wear. The boarding house had a reputation for being a clean and comfortable establishment, with breakfast and evening meals provided for guests.

Mrs. Wear was a small, friendly lady in her late Sixties who looked 10 years younger. Despite having lost her husband David five years ago, she carried on the Guest House single-handedly, well with the help of a local lady, Gladys, who helped with cleaning, washing, and doing anything else Mrs. Wear needed.

Tommy and the family were warmly greeted at the door and at once felt welcome by Mrs Wear. She showed them to their rooms which were on the 1st floor.

A Newcastle Lass

Liz Wear had been born and brought up in Byker, Newcastle, and she met her late husband, David, on a trip to Blackpool with her family when she was 18 years old.

David had a small boarding house in a back street in Blackpool with six letting rooms where Liz and her family stayed. Liz and David had an immediate connection, and one year later, they got married, and she became Mrs Clarke. Liz moved to Blackpool, and they ran the boarding house together until, sadly David died a few years ago from leukaemia. It was a blessing as he had really suffered and lost a tremendous amount of weight. He was a shadow of his former self.

David had a large life insurance that went to Liz, plus he had made a will and left everything, including the boarding house, to her.

Liz loved being a landlady, but the small boarding house held too many memories for her, it was time to move on. There was a large boarding house that was up for sale near the front. Liz viewed it… it was perfect but needed a woman's touch. She bought it with money from the insurance company and the sale of their boarding house. It took 6 months to bring the Guest House to the standard she envisaged.

She named it *THE CARVILLE GUEST HOUSE*.

(Carville being the name of the street in Newcastle where she was born and grew up in.) Above the front door was a sign "Owner and Proprietor… Elizabeth Wear." Liz had gone back to her maiden name.

The Carville had gained a good reputation, with visitors coming back every year. It was immaculate, beautifully decorated, with wonderful comfortable beds and the best of food.

Gladys was a great cook and helped with the breakfasts. Liz had hired a man called John to cook the evening meals during the peak tourist times in the Summer Season. He made wholesome and tasty food with no frills. Every night, the plates were empty; you would have thought the guests had licked them clean. Sign of a good cook!

The first floor had three bedrooms. They were all named after streets in Byker—Liz's hometown. Tommy and Isabella were in "Beresford," a double with a single for Mary Ellen, and Joan had "Clydesdale," a single small room and the four boys "Kendal," a family room, which had a double bed and 2 single ones. They were all spotlessly clean and decorated in pastel colours with matching curtains.

It was time for their dinner, so after getting washed in the first-floor bathroom, they went down to the dining room, which had a large window overlooking the front and a view of the sea. Mrs Wear has pushed three tables together so that the family could all sit together. The menu on the table was the choice of 2 evening dinners and 2 puddings, which were different each night. Tonight, there was chicken casserole with mashed potatoes and carrots or toad in the hole with chips. The puddings were apple crumble with custard or jelly with fruit and cream. The bairns chose the toad in the hole and the jelly and fruit. The adults were having the chicken and the apple crumble.

It all sounded delicious. Isabella and Joan were over the moon that they did not have to cook!

They all went to bed with full bellies, very tired from the journey and settled down in the lovely ever-so-clean beds. Within minutes, the bairns were asleep.

"Busy day tomorrow Issy. We will have to plan what we are going to do tomorrow at breakfast."

"Do not know about you lass, but I am so tired. I cannot keep my eyes open a minute longer." Before Isabella fell into a deep sleep, he kissed her goodnight. Tommy was snoring gently with the covers pulled up to his neck. Isabella was not long before she fell into a blissful sleep, thinking about the lovely week they were about to have.

Everyone was up quite early and ready for the day ahead, first breakfast, so down they all went to the Dining Room where Mrs. Wear was finishing setting the tables.

"Good morning, all, did you sleep well?" she asked.

"Out like a light, Mrs. Wear. Those beds of yours are comfortable, like sleeping on a cloud," replied Tommy.

"Thank you, I am so glad. You will be ready for your breakfast, what can I get you all?" It took a little while for everyone to decide what they wanted, but orders were taken, and Mrs. Wear headed off to the kitchen to give the order to Gladys, who was cooking today. Mrs. Wear made lots of tea and toast and took them to the table.

"Will not be long, please help yourself to cereal while you are waiting. The bairns all wanted cornflakes with milk and ate them very quickly as the hot breakfasts were beginning to arrive. The bairns ordered dippy eggs with soldiers, and the grown-ups had bacon, fried egg, sausage, beans, and fried bread. All looked and tasted delicious, and they told Mrs. Wear how good their breakfasts were and to please tell Gladys, too.

The week in Blackpool flew by. The bairns had a wonderful time playing on the beach most days, donkey rides, building sandcastles, paddling in the sea, hot chips at the Café by the beach, ice cream cones, and fizzy juice. The weather was good for the whole week there was sunshine every day but not too hot, and it was simply perfect.

Tommy, Isabella, and Joan enjoyed just sitting on a beach chair and watching all the kids on the beach having a wonderful time. Tommy and Isabella sometimes went for a walk together, leaving Joan in charge of the bairn. Joan adored Alex, Tommy Junior, and Mary Ellen as much as her boys, Michael, and Sean. They had become a family, and Joan could not believe how, just over a year ago, she was sitting on a similar beach where she met Isabella that day. In her mind Isabella was an angel sent by God to her when she was desperate and did not know which way to turn. Her thoughts were interrupted by Sean's shouting, "Hey Mam, come here and see what we have found." She went to where they were standing near the edge of the rocks.

They were discovering the rock pools nearby and found some Willicks which were clinging onto the rocks. They were little snail-like creatures which were boiled and picked out from their shells with a pin. A delicacy in the Northeast. Joan strolled over to where they were crowding around a rock pool. "Look Mam, it is a baby crab... Can we take it home, please? It has lost his Mam, and it looks lonely."

Joan tried not to laugh and said, "When the tide comes in, his Mam will be back looking for him, so he will be ok." With that sorted, off they went to dig some more holes and bury Michael.

All too soon, it was time to pack the cases and get the bus back to Newcastle. It has been a wonderful week for everyone, but good things do not last forever. But they all agreed that they would like to go back again; they loved Blackpool.

They said their goodbyes to Mrs. Wear, and Mary Ellen hugged her tightly.

"Aw lass, I will miss you, Mary Ellen. Now you be good for your Mam and Dad and I hope to see you all next year." She had a tear in her eye; this was just a wonderful family, and it was her pleasure to have them stay with her. She said her goodbyes to the rest of the family and gave Isabella a basket full of home baking for the bus journey.

"Thank you, Mrs Wear, this is just so kind and thoughtful of you."

Off they went, carrying their cases to the bus station, which was quite near for the journey home. Willy was waiting outside the bus, having a cigarette and a mug of tea when they arrived. "Hello, you lot, have you had a good time?" They all shouted, "Yes, we have," and got onto the bus to the seats that were booked for them.

When all the passengers were seated, Willie started the engine and said, "Okay, everyone seems to have had a fun time. Let us keep the holiday mood alive and sing all the way back to Newcastle." All the bairns on the bus shouted, "YES!" Of. course they only sang for an hour and ran out of songs they knew; it was thirsty work singing, so a stop at a local shop was for ice creams!'

They arrived back at Newcastle bus station late that night. Isabella's brother was there in Millie—the van, waiting for them.

Everyone was tired and went to bed straight away except Isabella and Joan who sat by the roaring fire which had been set by Isabella's brother before he picked them up at the bus station to warm the house through for them coming home.

Cases could wait to be unpacked and washing done tomorrow.

Chapter Twenty-Five
Joan's Story

Isabella and Joan sat by the fire, hugging their mug of strong tea. Joan said, "Isabella, I would like to thank you and Tommy for taking me, Michael, and Sean with you to Blackpool. We have never had a family holiday, and the boys have had the best time ever; I am just so grateful."

"Joan, it was nothing. Tommy and I both agreed that this would be a family holiday, and we regard you as a family now. You do so much for us, and our bairns just love you to bits. The twins are like older brothers, and we just love them to bits, too, so you deserve this," Isabella replied.

Joan had tears rolling down her cheeks; she thought of the life she and the boys had before all this.

"Joan do not cry. What it is, tell me."

"Isabella, you do not know how much it meant to us that day I met you in Tynemouth. You saved me and the twins that day. You deserve to hear my story. You took me in not knowing anything about me; you need to hear about my life before I met you."

They re-filled their mugs with tea, and Joan told Isabella her story.

Joan was married at 17 as she was pregnant. Her boyfriend was Jonny He lived on the next street to her family in Byker. Jonny had a bit of a reputation with the ladies; he was older at 22 and so handsome. She used to follow him unknowingly and one day, he turned around and saw her. "Hey lass, are you following me?" he said with a cheeky grin. Joan was blushing.

"You... wish," she responded.

Jonny had seen her for a few days, following him. She is quite pretty, he thought, obviously likes me, why not, it looks like she would be willing.

"Want to have a walk in the park?" he asked one day.

Joan blushed; he had asked her sort of out on a date, it was just a walk. She tried to hide her excitement; she had butterflies in her belly. She tried to sound not too eager, "Okay, I don't need to be home for another hour, so I suppose it will pass the time."

She is playing hard to get, thought Jonny, he loved that, the thrill of the chase, court them, flatter them, have his wicked way, and move on —another conquest he could brag about with his mates at the pub. They had a competition going on who could bed the most girls in the month. Jonny was out in the lead, but handsome Richie was catching up with another three added to his score last week.

A Newcastle Lass

Jonny and Joan walked through the park, chatting generally. Jonny asking all the right questions; it was a game to him, and he knew how to play it. There was a £10 note for the winner of bedding the most girls at stake, and he wanted to win. These girls should be paying him anyway; he was a catch, and any girl should feel grateful.

He arranged to take Joan to Whitley Bay on Sunday, which was tomorrow. There was no hanging about; he needed more scores quickly. Sunday came, and they went by train to Whitley Bay. Walked along the front hand in hand. "Want a bag of chips, Joan?" he asked.

"Please, can I have salt and brown sauce on them?"

"Nee bother lass, ye can have anything yer want," Jonny replied with a great big smile and a kiss on the lips. And went off to buy them. Joan was loving this date, and Jonny had kissed her too. After they had eaten their chips, they walked to the far end of the beach and for a walk along some of the coves. They lay down in one of these coves to listen to the waves and enjoy the sun. It was then he started to kiss her gently at first, which she enjoyed, but soon he became more demanding and aggressive. Joan did not realize that Jonny was on top of her, and then she felt the pain. It was all over in minutes, and he rolled off her. Joan was crying, and Jonny said, "It is only natural between boyfriend and girlfriend, and you were amazing!" She did not know which way to take that, and he said, "I have been with a few girls, Joan and believe me, you are the best!" That line worked for Joan, and she smiled that Jonny thought she was the best at lovemaking.

They took the train back home and he said he would be in touch. A whole month had passed, and Joan had not heard anything from him. She thought he must be busy at his work; he said he was going to work overtime to get extra money to treat her to a night out.

Another couple of weeks passed, and she realized her monthly period had not arrived. She told her mam about this, thinking she must have something wrong with her. Her mam asked if she had been seeing a boy and if he had done something to her, which Joan was not sure what she meant. Her mam took her to the doctor's that morning, and it was confirmed that Joan was pregnant.

Her mam and dad were angry at first, how could she do this to them? It was a disgrace to the family. Who was the boy, and where did he live? Joan was sobbing as her angry dad went to find Jonny and get him to do the right thing by his daughter or else.

My God, he had been well and truly caught; he had been lucky with the lasses up until now. He married Joan at the Registry Office within the month. Joan's Mam and Dad disowned her for bringing shame on them, and she had to go and live at Jonny's house, off Raby St., with his mam and dad in Byker, a two-bedroomed terrace house in Beresford Road, which was not the cleanest of places. His mam and dad took a disliking to her straight away, and although she tried to please them by cleaning and tidying the house, they were happy to live as they did.

"Stop all this cleaner; a bit of dirt never harmed anyone, anyway. Cannot find a thing these days," said the dad. "Aye, and another mouth to feed as well, I'll swing for that son of mine sowing his oats, dirty beggar." Joan stayed in their bedroom most of the time by herself. She could not do anything right with these people. Hopefully, Jonny will earn enough with all the overtime he works to afford a rented house for us and the baby soon.

She rarely saw her husband. He was away at the crack of dawn to his work at the railway sheds and did not often come home till 10 at night, sometimes smelling of beer. When she questioned him about spending their "rent money" on beer, he got angry and slapped her hard across one cheek. Joan started to cry, holding her cheek. "And stop that snivelling, woman! Can't a bloke have a pint after a hard day's work?" Jonny shouted at her.

She thought on that and nodded her head, " Sorry Jonny."

Irene Richardson

Chapter Twenty-Six
Jonny

This was now a regular thing. Jonny stayed out longer, and it did not seem to matter to him that his wife was now 8 months pregnant. And he took his frustration out on her, and she was beaten on a regular basis. His mam and dad did not interfere To them, it was his business, and they did not much care for Joan anyway, she had trapped their son. She deserved it anyway. They just turned the volume on the radio louder.

Joan went into labour a couple of weeks early. Brought on by one of Jonny's outbursts.

They got to the hospital just before she was ready to give birth and was rushed to the delivery room. Jonny left and went to see his mates at the pub. "Bloody Woman's Business, anyway," and off he went.

Joan delivered not just one but two healthy boys.

Jonny will love having two sons, she thought.

But he did not come to the hospital that night to see his sons or the next day either. Joan thought something dreadful had happened to him and now was starting to worry.

He eventually arrived 3 days later, smelling of beer and looking as though he had slept in his clothes. Joan was embarrassed as she knew he looked a mess, her husband turning up at the hospital 3 days after she had given birth. She could hear the whisperings in the ward. He was unaware that he had 2 boys until Joan told him. The Nurse brought the twins in their cot to the side of the bed for him to see. He looked at them and said, "Don't even look like me; you are sure they are mine?" Joan fought back the tears, how could he say such a thing, she was heartbroken.

"Have to go, meeting up with the lads for a game of darts, see you back at home when you get out," and with that, left without a kiss or anything.

All feelings she had for this man, the father of new baby boys, had gone out the window. She saw him for what he was, he did not love her or care about her feelings. What choice did she have. Her mam and dad had disowned her and wanted nothing to do with her or Jonny. They did not even know that they now had grandchildren. She wished she were dead, all she had now was her babies. Yes, she thought, they are my babies. He does not seem to want anything to do with them or me. She turned to her new twins and promised them she would try to give them the best she could. At this point, she did not know what would happen; all she knew was that she would never give them up. She cried herself to sleep; all seemed so hopeless.

Joan returned to Jonny's parents' house.

She had nowhere else to go with her babies, and she had no choice at all. She was dreading it.

Back to the squalor that they did not see or pretended not to see.

She had no choice but to make the best of it.

After a few months, Jonny had said that his mam and dad could not cope with them living there with two crying babies and they would have to find a place of their own. The news did not surprise Joan; she had been expecting this for a while. It was clear from the beginning they did not like her; they believed that she had trapped their son into getting married by getting pregnant and had ruined his life.

Ada and Bill Robertson would not have a word said against their son. He was their only son, and he looked after them.

Jonny, on the other hand, did not have the same feelings about them. They were leeches in his eyes. Taking whatever they could, he kept them in beer and cigarettes and paid the rent for them. His dad had never held down a job in his life; he was an alcoholic and was not a reliable employee, so any job he did manage to get did not last long. He turned up for work late or not at all. He really was not bothered about working, would rather stay at home all day. Both parents were lazy and did no cleaning as such; they preferred to lounge about all day.

Jonny, now at 23 now, was beginning to get really fed up with his life in general. He looked after his parents, who sucked him dry of every penny, they could out of him. He lived in squalor, now had a whimpering wife whom he had no feelings for and on top of that, she had produced two screaming brats.

Some of his friends evaded him as he was always bragging about his way with the lasses and and how he was trapped in a loveless marriage, not to mention the two babies crying and not sleeping, he was not the fun mate he used to be.

Now he had a big problem: his parents were wanting Joan and the babies out of the house. What was he to do. He still paid the rent for his mam and dad. Joan was doing his head in by saying he must find a place for them to live. All he really wanted was to get his old life back again.

Irene Richardson

Chapter Twenty-Seven
Uncle Jim

Jonny had a brain wave ... he would contact his Uncle Jim in Gosforth, who owned a lot of property in and around Newcastle and Gateshead, and he would ask for his help. He had not seen him since he was 15 years old. Uncle Jim's wife had died, and she was his mam's sister, so they went to the funeral. Uncle Jim was nice to him at the funeral and said he would come to him if he needed a job as he had contacts. He never took up his generous offer. His Mam and Dad were left £150 in the will, which was soon spent.

He decided to see Uncle Jim the next week. He lived in a large stone house with a big garden in a posh area of Gosforth. Uncle Jim was expecting Jonny as he had written him a letter.

"Come in lad; my you have grown. Sarah will make us a cup of tea; it is freezing out there." They went through to the front room, which was about as big as Jonny's whole house.

They had general chit-chat until Sarah came back with a tray of tea and biscuits. Sarah was Uncle Jim's housekeeper and kept things running ship-shape.

Over tea, Jonny explained how he was now the proud Dad of two beautiful boys and a wife called Joan. How his parents wanted them out of the house and, how he paid their rent, etc., and to ask if he had a spare small house available to help them out for a while until he got back on his feet.

Uncle Jim thought for a moment. "Jonny, I have always been fond of you. Your mam was my little sister whom I adored Unfortunately, she fell for a waster of a man and apart from having you, her life has been on a downward slope. She had given up trying to reform your dad over the years and accepts that life is the way it is, and nothing is going to change. I am proud that you have paid their rent for them. I do not know if you have been told that their house belongs to me. Over the years, I have put the rent money you have paid for them into an account for you to give you at some crisis in your life. I think that time has come today, I can afford not to take any rent from my sister and give the money back to you that you have paid in rent these last few years. If I remember right, it was about 800 pounds. This would give you, your wife, and your bairns a good start.

"I have no houses to rent at the moment, but I know a landlord who has a 2 bedroomed terrace house unfurnished, going in Walker, needs a bit of doing up, but the rent is cheap, and you will have this money to do it up and buy some furniture. What do you say?"

Jonny was speechless; this was the answer to his problem. He would not sort out Joan and the twins at once, but he will have to put up with them in the meantime.

"I cannot thank you enough Uncle Jim, I am grateful for this. Wait till I get home and tell Joan. She will be over the moon to have her own place. We can be a real family." He shook Uncle Jim's hand and thanked him again.

"I will contact the landlord that I mentioned and will let you know. I am sure it will be all right. You would best be getting off; it is starting to get late, and your wife will have your tea ready. "

"I'm sure she will She is a good cook and she is a wonderful mam to the twins too."

Lying came easily for him. Said his goodbye to Uncle Jim, and off he went, whistling all the way home with the £800.

Of course, he did not tell Joan about the money but had said he visited his uncle to see if he had house to rent for them. He did not but knew a man who had a 2 bedroom in Walker, and it seemed a dead cert he would let him know soon. Joan was just so happy thinking that he was trying to get them a home of their own. She needed to get out of this place and hope to God she would not have to see his parents again. They did not like her anyway and had nothing to do with the twins. Jonny told Joan about the house for rent in Walker he was just waiting for his uncle to see the landlord and to know when they could view it.

A Newcastle Lass

The following week, they were standing at the door of the house for rent. It looked a bit run down to Joan. The landlord, Robert Davies, answered the door to them. "Come in and have a look around" he said. It could do with a lick of paint, but overall, a solid house and rent is reasonable.

They were astounded by the amount of work that needed doing, but Jonny could do the work.

"We'll take it," says Jonny without even consulting Joan. "When can we get the keys?"

Joan walked through the rest of the house, it felt dark and gloomy.

Light paint on the walls would do the trick though and we will need some bits of furniture.

Jonny paid the deposit of £50 in cash from the money he had gotten from Uncle Jim and was then given the keys.

The landlord Mr. Davies said he would collect the rent of £2.3s.6p. a week every Friday afternoon. He was a short man with a pot belly, thin black hair sleeked back with Brylcream and a pencil-thin black moustache. He looked like the gangsters in the films. Joan did not like him; he was what you call "smarmy?" Yes, that would describe him best, "Smarmy."

Jonny got to work on the house, with the help of some friends fixing, replacing, and decorating, laying lino, and getting some nice secondhand furniture for the living room and a three-piece suite in a dark green velvet material for only £25; it was new. A rug for the fireplace, crockery, cutlery, pots, pans, a double bed, and some bedding. A mixture of towels too. These were bought very cheaply from a friend and his wife, who were emigrating to Australia on the £10 ticket offer. So had to sell all their household items. He had only spent about £60 on everything and was feeling chuffed with himself.

Jonny was good to his word and, with the help of a few mates, had the place looking good.

Joan thought he had changed and was a happy family man... how wrong could she be?

Her husband was never home much these days; he was always out with his mates, and she stayed at home with the twins.

And so was Joan's life. Jonny did give her housekeeping money, although not much, but she was careful with it. He paid the rent too. The twins, Sean, and Michael were now 4 years old and did not really know their dad. He went out before they were up in the morning and were bathed and fast asleep in bed when he decided to come home. Often drunk and smelling of cheap perfume.

She made the mistake of asking him where he had been and whose perfume was on his clothes Jonny looked at her scathingly and was getting angrier by the minute.

His answer to that was a good beating. Joan had to be careful; he had mood swings and got angry at the least little thing, and she got the brunt of his fists.

All was well for about two years; she did not see much of him, but that was fine with her.

Then one day, Jonny just got up and left. He wrote a quick note to say he had met someone else and was moving to Scotland with her. Joan was mortified; she had some money put aside for a rainy day. And wondered how long it would last her. Fridays were a total nightmare; the Landlord came around three for his rent money. Joan had to make some excuses that Jonny had not left it and would pay double next week. But she was now in serious arrears, and the landlord had said she had to pay what was due next week in full or move out He also hinted about paying him in "kind" if she knew what that meant! Joan knew what he meant and shuddered at the thought.

"I would rather be homeless than be beholden to this creep of a man." Joan did not know what to do and, with a little money left, took the twins to Tynemouth for the day, just to escape what was going on. "That was the day we met you!" said Joan.

"You were like an angel sent from heaven that day. I thought we would have had to go into the workhouse or sleep on the streets. I would not be able to get a job as I had the twins. I was just so desperate, so I used the last of my money to go to Tynemouth for the day to give the boys a lovely day before whatever lay ahead of us in Newcastle." Joan had tears rolling down her cheeks; when she looked at Isabella, she was the same. The two women hugged each other for a minute. Isabella thought how brave Joan was and so glad she and Tommy were there on the beach at Tynemouth that day.

As the years passed, Joan and her boys became part of the family, and life was good on both sides. Their two families became one, and life was good.

A Newcastle Lass

Chapter Twenty-Eight
Love at last

Joan had met a man called John who came from Gateshead. They met in Newcastle at a bus stop; they got chatting. John said he had been waiting at the bus stop for half an hour, and he was freezing and was going to get a cup of tea at a nearby cafe. Would she like to join him as the bus must have broken down or something, and it would be a while before the next one came. Joan said she would love a cup right now as it was a freezing day. They chatted over their tea for about two hours and did not realize the time.

John asked if he could see her again, and Joan thought he was a nice man, so yes, she would. They did meet up the following week and found they had a lot in common. John told her that his wife had died 5 years ago with a brain tumour and really did not go out much these days.

John and Joan met up once a week over the following six months and John asked Joan to marry him and move in with him. Joan said yes after she had talked it over with Isabella, who was just so happy for her. She was welcome to visit at any time as not just a friend but also a member of the family. John and Joan married the following week As John said, "Why wait Joan, let us enjoy every day we have!"

The twins also moved into John's house which had four bedrooms, and they got on with John and thought he was perfect for their mam. She had come alive for the first time ever!

They all settled into John's s house quickly, but it oneeded redecorated. It had not been done for years. John told Joan to go ahead with the work and he agreed as it was looking slightly shabby. She had a fun time buying paint, wallpaper, curtains, and carpets. It took a few months to finish, but the result was amazing.

John was a quiet man and very loving too, and he could not believe how lucky he was to have found Joan. He had never thought he would ever get married again. He had a wonderful marriage to his former wife. She was the opposite of Joan in terms of looks, manners, and personality. She was a quiet person who enjoyed staying at home, whereas Joan was outgoing and bubbly.

John enjoyed going on holidays down to the Lake District, Devon and Cornwall, and his wife liked to stay at home so when she went on holiday, she was always ready to come back home after a couple of days.

John asked Joan about going on holiday; she got quite excited and said, "Yes, please." Opposite to his former wife.

A Newcastle Lass

John and Joan planned quite a few holidays, and the first one was to visit the Lake District. They packed the car and set off. They visited Windermere and Bowles's, Ullswater, Keswick, Ambleside, staying overnight at a Bed and Breakfast Accommodation.

The weather was good, except for one day when they had arranged a boat trip on Lake Windermere, when it was pouring. They were soaked, but they just laughed and made the most of it. They loved each other's company and not even the weather could dampen their spirits.

Irene Richardson

Chapter Twenty-Nine
Mary Ellen

Mary Ellen, at 13, still had another year left at school and really did not know which job to pick. She changed her mind daily.

Her schoolwork was good, not brilliant, but sufficient to get her a decent job.

When Mary Ellen eventually left school, she decided that she wanted to work in a shop. Like her mam she loved to talk to people. She got a job in a local Grocers which Isabella and Tommy were not too pleased about. Mary Ellen was following her heart, not her head. She could have gotten a much better job, nursing, junior in an office, or a hairdresser (she was good with hair), but no, the shop assistant was her choice.

Mary Ellen's customers just loved her, and they spent more time talking to her than doing their shopping. The owner, Mrs Craigs, had to have a word with her to remind her that sometimes there was a queue and people who did not like waiting! So be aware of this, Mary Ellen. Mrs. Craig thought that Mary Ellen was doing an excellent job but had to remind her this was a shop and not a social club.

It was one day that a handsome lad came into the shop to buy some Woodbines and a box of matches; he liked what he saw. Mary Ellen was a good-looking lass; he would chat her up.

His name was Albert Hogg, and he lived in Byker in Brock Street along with his dad and mam, four brothers: Christopher, Norman, Sydney, Willie and one sister: Irene. They were crowded into two bedrooms, with another bed in the living room for the parents. This was the best bed in the house as the coal fire in the cast iron fireplace was burning constantly. The brothers only had a year between them in age, and all their clothes fitted one another. The first one up in the morning got the pick of the clothes that his mam Polly, had washed and ironed the night before. Albert was the dapper one he had a reputation as being a ladies' man, so he needed to wear the best of the newly washed clothes. Albert took after his dad, Geordie. He was always dressed in a suit, a starched collar on his shirt, a tie, and a trilby hat. Geordie walked tall and straight. When he was younger, he was in the Scot's Guards a very smart regiment with extremely exacting standards of dress, a habit he continued all his life.

Albert just loved to go to the Dance Hall; he was an incredibly good dancer and waltzed the ladies around the floor effortlessly. He also got to hold them close and could feel the outline of their curves.

Some women did not mind this at all, but some pulled away feeling embarrassed. He never asked the latter to dance again; there were plenty of others to choose from.

Albert was not one for settling down with one woman and made sure they got the message. Some liked to think they could be his girlfriend, but little did they know Albert had little to offer and if he were to settle down, it would be with a woman who had money to keep him.

So here he was, staring at Mary Ellen across the counter, waiting on his Woodbines and matches. He normally rolled his own tabs (cigarettes)as it was much cheaper, but he had just been paid and was splashing out. Mary Ellen was a shy girl, had not had many boyfriends in the past, and relationships were mostly a cuddle and a kiss. She wanted to keep herself chaste for the man she would marry, just as her mam had done. Isabella had told her the basic unpleasant facts, so there would be no surprises when she did marry.

Mary Ellen liked the look of this man who was smiling at her across the counter. He looked like the film star Clark Gable! She was blushing. He took out one of his cigarettes and lit it up with a match from the packet he had just bought. "Want one?" he asked, holding out the Woodbines.

"Don't smoke," she said.

"Do not know what you are missing pet, try one," and he lit it for her. Mary Ellen almost choked, and Albert said, "First one is always like that." He went on his way, trying not to show her his interest, keep her on her toes. He laughed, she could do the running.

Mary Ellen quite liked the attention she got from Albert; little did she know what he was really like that she would find out in time.

Mary Ellen did not see Albert for a while and thought he must not be interested in her. She had started going out with a lad from Conyers Road. His name was James; they used to know each other at school. They went for long walks holding hands and the odd kiss. It was a nice friendship, and they enjoyed each other's company. It was not serious, and although Mary Ellen liked James, he was a bit boring and predictable she was looking for a bit more excitement.

James was a lovely, well-mannered young man, but his idea of a romantic date was to sit in the back row of the picture house, watch a film holding hands and kiss goodnight when he took her home. He was not a good kisser either; just shut his eyes and mouth and pressed his lips against hers for all of 5 seconds. She wanted to be kissed like the women in the movies until she was breathless! Be courted and swept off her feet like Clark Gable; she swooned over him.

She wanted to be taken dancing, on a day trip to the seaside, ride on the back of a motorbike, swim in the sea, have a picnic with a blanket on the grass, be told how beautiful she was, be loved passionately, be given flowers and chocolates, run barefoot in the rain in a meadow? The problem with Mary Ellen was that she read too many romantic novels and was naïve to believe this is what courtship was all about.

She thought that she would die an old housekeeper.

Irene Richardson

Chapter Thirty
Albert

Albert was enjoying his life as a womanizer. He enjoyed the thrill of chasing a woman, although he need not have tried hard. He had that air of pretending he was not interested if he saw someone he liked and ignored them. This was his successful ploy, and it worked every time. The more he ignored them, the more they were interested.

He had to be more careful these days with whom he had sex with as he had caught a few "contagious intimate diseases" which were dealt with at a clinic. Fortunately, had been lucky, and these had been treated successfully.

His younger brother, Norman and him, played guitar and sang Country and Western songs in some of the local pubs. They were known as The Hogg Brothers. Being in the limelight made him popular with the women. He could choose whom he bedded from the audience where they were playing.

Albert was a wood machinist to trade. He loved working with wood and creating. He was offered a contract in Africa for a year to train the local employees on the new machines during the initial setup of a factory. After the year was up, he came back to Newcastle, leaving a few offspring there.

Within the first week of getting home, he bumped into Mary Ellen. He remembered the shy girl from the grocers he met a long time ago.

She was young and pretty back then when he first met her, but too young for him at that time. It was over two years since then. He had not been interested then because of her age, but it was a different story now.

This was now a challenge for him.

"Hello, he said, don't I know you?" Mary Ellen was flattered that he remembered her. She certainly remembered him. He had sleeked-back Brylcreamed hair and a mustache like Clark Gable, not as handsome, but close.

He stared at her with his piercing blue eyes…. She was quite mesmerized. "Well, we briefly met when I was working in Mrs. Craig's, a few years back. How are you?"

"Yes, you tried your first cigarette and nearly threw up on me." Mary Ellen laughed.

"I now smoke about 10 a day, your fault," she punched his arm.

"How about I take you out to make up for it?" says Albert.

Mary Ellen said nothing; she was in a daze.

Albert knew how to play this. "Okay, no bother," and started to walk away.

"I suppose it would be nice, alright then."

As usual, it worked. Show them you are not really bothered and watch it happen.

"You like dancing?" She nodded. "Right then, it's a date, meeting you here on Saturday at 7, okay?" And off he went down the road whistling to himself. Some fella, you are Albert! Scored again!

Saturday came, and Albert dressed in his one and only suit, which he had bought in the second-hand shop. It was a bargain and almost new. His mam had washed and ironed his white shirt and a borrowed a blue striped tie from his dads' collection that completed the look.

Looking quite dapper, off he went, sure of himself and knew he would have his way with her tonight. His dates always let him. This one was no different, well a bit more of the "Albert Charm" needed, but it worked every time.

Mary Ellen was nervous about her date. Albert was older and more worldly wise, or so she thought. Would he think that she was as too young and naive?

She chose a pale blue dress, which was the same colour as her eyes. Had washed her brunette hair and clipped the sides back with two silver slides. She checked herself in the mirror before she left. Oh my, she was feeling excited and nervous at the same time.

Albert was waiting for her where they arranged to meet. He looked very handsome in his suit and was ever so smart.

A Newcastle Lass

They arrived at the dance hall and put their coats on the check-in desk.

"How about a drink? What would you like?" Albert asked.

"Just an orange juice, please." Albert ordered her an orange juice, and unbeknown to her, with some gin in it and he had a beer.

Mary Ellen had a fun time, and by the time the dance hall was losing, she was feeling very tipsy with all the "extra gin."

Albert walked her home via the park and went through the gates to a little clearing in the bushes he knew quite well. He started to kiss her neck and fondled her breasts. She did not stop him as it felt nice. She had not gone this far before with any boy. Albert was used to older women, and it was a new experience for her. Albert knew she had no experience of lovemaking with her dates; they were all young boys, he would teach her. Although she was enjoying the kissing and cuddling, things were getting a bit more serious. Albert had a hand in her pants. At first, she enjoyed this; the gin had relaxed her, but as Albert became more aroused, she began to panic and tried to push his hand away. Before she knew it, he had pushed her down on the grass and lay on top of her. She felt a sharp pain down below, and Albert took no notice of her asking him to stop. He kept thrusting for a couple of minutes, groaned, and got off her. "That was good for me, Mary Ellen. Was it good for you?"

She was crying, and he was not even taking any notice, it seemed like all this to him was normal, and she should be enjoying it. She had a lot to learn.

Irene Richardson

Over the next couple of months, Albert dated Mary Ellen and enjoyed having sex with her. She was starting to enjoy it, or so he thought.

Chapter Thirty-One
Albert

A couple of months later, she told Isabella, her mam, that she had missed her monthly period. Of course, she was pregnant, and of course it was Albert's. Time to talk to him, so Isabella got in touch, and Albert came for tea the following Sunday. He had his suspicions of why he was invited.

The following Sunday, he dressed smartlly, needed to make an impression, he thought.

Tommy answered the door, "Better come in, lad," and he led the way to the living room where Isabella and Mary Ellen were sitting.

There was a tea tray on the table, and the 4 places had been set with cups, saucers, and small plates. There was a large fruit cake in the centre waiting to be cut.

Albert glanced around and made a mental note that these folk were well off, and he smiled to himself. Good catch here, let us hear what they have to say, no doubt a lecture on how to treat their daughter.

They sat at the table, ate the cake, and drank their tea in silence; it was awkward. Tommy started to ask Albert questions about where he worked and lived and about his family, all personal stuff, which made Albert a bit wary. Obviously as parents, they wanted to see if any young man was good enough for them and their daughter.

Albert told a few white lies, some things that he thought they would like to hear otherwise he would be considered unsuitable and thrown out the door.

After the tea things were cleared away, they went to sit at the fireside. Tommy had a serious look on his face. "Now lad, we have asked you to come here to make some plans about you and our Mary Ellen. She is having your baby, and you will do the decent and right thing by marrying her as soon as possible."

Albert thought, he had better keep the old man sweet, so he said, "Thank you. I am ever so grateful to you and Mrs. Taylor, and I promise to take good care of your daughter."

This sounded good to Albert, and he was quite chuffed with his quick thinking. He sounded like an ideal, caring son-in-law, nothing could be further from the truth. Tommy knew Albert was lying through his teeth, cocky bastard, so he was, but a new wife and baby to look after may just be the making of him.

"Okay, Albert, we may have misjudged you, but if you promise to look after our Mary Ellen and the baby, then you have our blessing. It is not what we would have liked for Mary Ellen's future, but we will help you both, providing you work towards supporting your wife and family, then we will be happy enough with that.

"Now enough said about that, let us get this wedding planned quickly, not a big grande affair, but close friends and family only.

"You and Mary Ellen can make a list of people to invite. My Isabella is a dab hand at planning things, and I am sure she will do her best for you both.

"Now future son-in-law and dad-to-be, how about we open a couple of beers and a couple of sweet sherries for the ladies?"

Tommy Junior, and Alex had been banished for an hour, so they went for a walk. Just at that point, they all came in tentatively looking at their faces and saw Tommy, Albert, Isabella, and Mary Ellen with a drink in their hands. Thank God, everything must have gone ok. "Get yourselves a drink and join us," says Tommy

Albert just could not stop smiling, what just happened?

Cannot believe it is going to be all right. He did not love Mary Ellen or want a crying bairn, but with money and a house he would be ok. That daft old beggar Tommy believed him; what a fool!

Little did Albert know, but Tommy was not a daft old fool and knew exactly what the score was with Albert. He was no fool by any means. He would be keeping a close eye on him for sure. He was doing this for his daughter, Mary Ellen.

Isabella rushed about like a mad woman organizing her daughter's wedding. She would try to give her the beautiful wedding she deserved but not spending a lot of money. After all, Tommy was also providing them with a house and rent for a year. Just as well he has a decent job, but any savings had to be kept for when he retires.

Albert and Mary Ellen were married at the Registrars in Newcastle. The ceremony only took 15 minutes, not what Isabella wanted for her only daughter. She had envisioned a beautiful white wedding attended by friends and family. A wedding reception afterwards in a pleasant hotel. Mary Ellen dressed in a beautiful blue two-piece suit with a matching hat. Albert, her husband to be in his suit, so in love and ready to start a wonderful, happy life together.

But Albert would put an end to Isabella's dreams for her daughter. Daft woman, she thought the sun shone out of Mary Ellen's arse!

The two families went for afternoon tea in Newcastle after the Registrars to a hotel near the Newcastle Central Railway Station for afternoon tea to celebrate. Albert's parents, George and Polly and his brother Norman, who acted as Best Man, went. Albert thought that it was all very "poncy" and a waste of an afternoon, never mind the cost! But that was the way Albert thought; why did he not have money? Why did he not have or get any good luck… he had a huge chip on his shoulder, and the entire entire world owed him a living!

Everyone was civil to each other. Tommy and Isabella tried their best to be happy for the couple. But in their minds, they knew that Albert was not right. Tommy had found them a two-bedroomed terrace house in Shipley Street opposite the Shipley Wash House, Swimming Pool, and the Public Baths, where you could have a hot deep bath. Soap and a towel were extra. The bath was made of stoneware and was very deep, a place to luxuriate in peace for a while.

The swimming pool was popular with all ages. The water was freezing, but not too bad if you swam faster. There was a three-tiered diving board, and all the local lads jumped off the top one to impress the giggling girls in the shallow end.

The Wash House was a hub of activity all day long, women from Byker went to do their washing in the big metal sinks, which was extremely exhausting as their family clothes were dirty. Many of the husbands had manual jobs in the coal mines, docks, and the Engineering Works, so a lot of coal dust and engine oil, which needed to be scrubbed with a bar of washing soap, a hard brush, and a metal corrugated washboard. The water had to be changed several times.

Then the clothes had to be put through the rollers of a big mangle. Lastly, they hung their washing in the heated dryers, which were tall, pull-out rails. The clothes, when loaded onto the rails, would be pushed back into the hot dryer openings.

While the clothes were drying, the women congregated together to gossip; many friendships were formed here.

They sat on benches with each other, chatting and laughing and gossiping about someone or another until the clothes were dry. The woman loaded their clean, dry clothes into their form of transport, which was usually in a tin bath loaded onto a pram chassis and pushed their heavy load back home to iron.

A washing was usually done once a week. This was a hard, backbreaking job, but it had to be done. You certainly could not survive if you were a weakling; these women were strong!

Albert George Hogg was a moody man. When things were ok, he was bright and cheerful. He could be the life and soul of a party. He had mood swings, which left Mary Ellen confused.

He was not about much during her pregnancy. When not working, he would still act like a single-person bloke getting dressed and going out with his friends for a few beers.

Mary Ellen gave birth to a daughter in Nov 1938 while he was out with his friends. It was a girl, and they had decided to call her Brenda.

Albert seemed to settle down a bit when he became a new dad, but like everything else, his good intentions went out the window. That was the story of Albert's life. He never stuck at anything long, lost interest and moved on to something else.

Albert was a wood machinist to trade; he enjoyed working with all kinds of wood and even made some of the furniture in their house.

A Newcastle Lass

Mary Ellen was left alone to look after baby Brenda. She was a happy baby and smiled a lot. Albert used to go to the Raby Pub with his brother Norman. They played guitar and sang Country and Western songs, and the folk used to put money in a pint glass they had beside them. On a good night, they could get a few pounds each. Mary Ellen did not see a penny of this; he kept it to himself. He had earned it in his mind.

Albert did not hold a job down long. He always thought there was something better ahead. So, he would start a job somewhere and thought he knew better how to do things, so he ended up falling out with workmates and bosses. He had a big chip on his shoulder.

He unfortunately had a bit of a short fuse and often took it out on Mary Ellen, getting into an argument with her over trivial things. When he got home, he expected to have his dinner waiting and ready. After all, he was the breadwinner and kept reminding her. It amounted to mental abuse.

Irene Richardson

Chapter Thirty-Two
The Date Factory

Great Britain was at war with Germany, and healthy males had to enlist to serve in the armed forces. Albert joined the Army and was away for a while.

While Albert was away in the Army, serving his country, Mary Ellen got a part-time job at the local Date Factory at the top of Carville Road and Cheviot View.

The factory was a good place to work during the war, the women who worked there were a jolly lot. Mary Ellen looked forward to her day there in a happy place.

The women used to sing all day; one started with a popular song, and everyone else joined in. Then someone else had a favourite and started the next song. Popular ones were Vera Lynn, The Mills Brothers especially, "You Always Hurt The One You Love," "Boogie, Woogie, Bugle Boy" by the Andrews Sisters and "Sentimental Journey" by the lovely Doris Day.

The supervisor, Davey, oversaw this bunch of women. He secretly enjoyed all their singing and often joined in when he thought no one was looking. One day they got him to sing his favourite "I'll Be Seeing You." Davey had a beautiful voice, and the women stopped what they were doing to listen to him. They clapped and cheered when he finished.

The women loved to play tricks on poor Davey. He had the same routine every day. At 7.55, he would go to his hook on the factory wall where he hung his brown working overalls and his wellingtons that lay underneath on the floor. He changed into his "working clothes" for the day. Boy, was he in for a surprise.

The women were in before him and sewed together the hem of each leg of his trousers and put a layer of dates in the soles of his wellingtons that squelched when he put them on.

The women were in hysterics at his efforts to get his feet into the trousers, then the wellingtons that were gooey with squashed dates. When Davey put his feet into his wellingtons, they were gross! And there were a few choice words thrown at them, "No bloody tea break for you lot today, and you'll not be eating any of those dates either, I'll be keeping an eye on you."

"Yes Sir, Sergeant Major," they all chanted back, and they broke into hysterical laughter all over again, Secretively Davey thought it was hilarious too, but was not letting on. These women made his day. Davey went off to the washroom to tidy up and get the sticky dates off his feet, off his hands and he had rubbed his face too. Little did Davey know, but some of the women had put a few drops of red cochineal in the soap dispenser.

When Davey came out of the washroom, he looked like a Red Indian! The laughter lasted for ages; they had really aching bellies with the joke! Mind you, so did Davey!

Davey had lost his wife to cancer over two years ago. He helplessly watched her struggle with her illness; it was a cruel existence for her. He tried as best he could but felt useless against the wasting disease. He did everything for her, from preparing her food to bathing and feeding her. After a prolonged illness, she passed away peacefully in her sleep. Davey was distraught; he had lost his beautiful, wonderful wife. His soulmate.

They had no children, so it was back to an empty house for him after work. The women in the factory did not know it but they were a lifesaver to him, and that was why he did not mind their games and sometimes, being at the sharp end of their antics.

Mary Ellen loved her job, well more the company of the women, they all became friends.

Albert's Mam, Polly, looked after Brenda while Mary Ellen went to work part-time 3 days a week.

The women organised a Bus Trip to the seaside every year. They paid a little each week into the fund for the hire of the bus and bought their lunch too at a local café. This has been booked at a café on the seafront for 40 people. Only one person could not make it as she was attending her husband's funeral. One of the women joked, "Sandra would have been better off on the bus trip; her man Billy was a miserable old beggar, and they had not been getting on for ages." It was sad times like this that the Date Factory Women pulled together in times of trouble and need. Newcastle Lasses were strong and resilient but also helpful, good friends, and stuck together like glue through thick and thin.

Irene Richardson

Chapter Thirty-Three
The Bus Trip

This year it was decided unanimously that Whitley Bay was the Bus Trip this year.

Each year they all made a hat to wear and the winner for the best or unusual one got £1. Ginny Hanson was the competitive one; her hats were a work of art and always had a theme. One year was the Mad Hatters Tea Party. Another was Punch and Judy. The women could not wait to see this year's one. Everyone looked forward to Ginny's creations.

Mary Ellen looked forward to making this year's hat for the Bus Trip. She had an old sun hat that belonged to her Mam, that would do nicely… It was a Sandy colour which made her think of the beach, so that was the inspiration for her seaside hat. Brenda had a box full of shells she had collected last time they went to the beach, and Mary Ellen borrowed them along with some green and blue ribbons which she would curl into waves. Her hat cost her nothing. She was proud of what she had made.

The day of the bus trip came, and all the women and Davey piled onto the bus. They were all wearing their hats, including Davey's, which had beer bottle tops glued on all over.. So original.

There were a lot of women who had sewn on ribbons in bright colours. And others with flowers sewn on, one was a snow scene made with lots of cotton wool.

Everyone thought that Mary Ellen's beach scene was good. The bus driver was to be the judge and chose Dave's beer bottle tops as the best original one. Dave's had earned him the one-pound prize money. "That should cover the cost of the beer I had to drink to get the bottle caps," Davey said jokingly.

They all were in a "Happy holiday mood," a lovely day off once a year, and they were going to enjoy it. Forget what was back at home; they were free for one day!

They all got off the bus to go to the café they had booked tables to have lunch for 40 of them. They were starving and very thirsty with all the singing they did at the top of their voices on the bus.

Lunch eaten, they split up to mooch around the town. There was not much to see, then they set off to the beach to have a paddle on the cold North Sea, and a little sleep on a deck chair, having been up early for their trip. Some of the women played a game of rounders, and before longing it was time to get back on the bus.

All done with their hats on!

Irene Richardson

Homeward bound, very tired, but had a lovely trip, great company, good workmates… roll on next year. Some were thinking about ideas for their hats already!

Back home, as they were getting off the bus, everyone put a couple of coppers into the driver's tip tray. Everyone said their goodbyes and went home to enjoy the rest of the weekend.

A Newcastle Lass

Chapter Thirty-Three
War ended

Little Brenda was growing fast and spent most of her younger years at her grandma's house. Grandma Polly who lived in Brock Street, just loved having her around.

Brenda did not know her Dad when he came home from the war. She was 7 years old now and was a bit stubborn; this she inherited from Albert.

A few months after Albert had come home, Mary Ellen found that she was pregnant. The baby was due in December.

There were a lot of babies born at the same time!

Husbands returning after the war.

Some wives and girlfriends had babies by soldiers who were stationed near Newcastle during the war and had to explain this addition to the family to their returning husbands and boyfriends.

Mary Ellen's Mam, Isabella, was over the moon at the thought of another grandchild. She started to knit some clothes for it. A December baby needs to be kept warm. She knitted wool blankets, mittens, booties suits, and hats. Baby Hogg would be the warmest and best-dressed baby in Byker!

Mary Ellen visited her Mam as much as she could, they were always close. Isabella took delight in showing Mary Ellen what she had been knitting, she was a beautiful knitter making all sorts of clothes for her new Grandchild. Isabella loved these visits from Mary Ellen and her Granddaughter Brenda, whom she adored even though she was a stubborn little miss with a pout to match if she did not get her own way. But Isabella could always get her on the side with a sweetie.

Brenda would enjoy going to her grandma's too as she always got something new to wear, a knitted cardigan or a dress made especially for her, not to mention Grandma was a brilliant baker who always had cake, jam tarts, apple pie or fresh hot scones from the oven. She even got some to take home in a brown paper bag and there were always a few pennies in the bottom. Brenda used to think which sweets she would buy tomorrow; her favourite was sherbet which came in a paper cone, and you dipped your finger in. Lemon was the best, but whichever flavour you had, your finger was always stained bright yellow!

Winters in the Northeast were harsh. December, January, and February brought heavy snow; most people stayed indoors.

Isabella kept a roaring coal fire going all day. The coal bucket by the side of the fire was empty. Time to get more coal for the coal bucket to top up the fire before it gets dark. Off she went to the coal shed to fill the bucket. It was freezing outside, and she quickly filled the bucket and hurried back to the Fire.

Isabella tripped on the rug in front of the fire and fell headfirst into the red-hot coals, burning her face. Tommy was just coming through the front door and heard her screams. He rushed into the living room and dragged her free. Most of her face was burned. She spent the next two months in hospital but, due to the seriousness of her injuries, unfortunately died.

Tommy was inconsolable; he loved her so much. He was just so lost without her. No way on earth could he face the future without her. She was his rock, his soulmate.

All their family, friends, and neighbours attended the funeral.

It was Isabella's wishes to be buried in Heaton Cemetery.

Her family were all buried there.

Everyone was more than welcome to go back to the house for tea and sandwiches. It was a sad day for everyone who knew this wonderful, kind, and caring lady who was a devoted wife, mother, and grandma.

Irene Richardson

A Poem for my Great Grandmother Isabella

A wife, a mother and grandma too…
This is the legacy we have from you,
You gave your love and selflessness,
You gave your strength and kindness
A stronger person would be hard to find,
And in your heart, you were always kind.
Not just as a wife, not just as a mother,
A loving grandmother, like no other
Rest in peace Isabella, you've earned your sleep
You live in my heart, memories if you I keep

Life carried on as usual for Mary Ellen; she had to think of her unborn baby and not stress it or herself.

Her daughter, Brenda was going to be 8 this year, and Mary Ellen had to put on a brave face for her daughter's sake. She was too young to fully understand. Brenda spent most of her days at Granny Polly's house, so she was not aware too much of what was happening.

Her Mam would never get the chance to see or hold her new grandchild. Losing her mam was just unbearable, but going into a depression was not the answer. Time was a great healer, everyone said, but you do not get over a loss like that.

Albert was of no comfort to her; he had no sympathy for her either, and now he had to put up with her crying and getting depressed. "Pull yourself together, woman. You are not the only one who has lost a parent." This was the last straw for Mary Ellen. She grabbed a vase near to her and threw it at Albert; it grazed his forehead. He was livid, shouted at her and stormed out of the house, leaving Mary Ellen sobbing even more.

He was spending more evenings out; Mary Ellen heard rumors about him being with other women and decided to ask him when he eventually got home.

It was 4 days before he showed his face. He was disheveled, dirty, and smelled of alcohol. Looking sheepish and deeply sorry for himself. He pleaded with Mary Ellen that he had learned his lesson and would try to be a better husband and dad.

How could she confront him when he was like this? She fetched fresh clothes for him and told him to get a wash. "I will have some dinner ready for you when you are done. Then we must talk." Albert for the first time in his life, did as he was told without an argument.

Mary Ellen made some fried egg and bacon with three slices of fried bread and a big Mug of strong tea for him when he came back to the kitchen table. Mary Ellen felt sorry for him, where had he been? What had he been doing? So many questions. Will let him tell me in his own time, but Albert never did.

Albert heard of a job as a cabinet maker with a small, specialised business on City Road, run by a Cockney guy from London by the name of Alec Turner.

Irene Richardson

Chapter Thirty-Four
Alec

Alec was looking for someone with an eye for good, solid furniture, made cheaply but had the look of something expensive. On his way to an interview, Albert laughed to himself, "Cheaply made but looks expensive! I like that; describes me, ha ha."

Albert and Alec hit it off right away, Alec could see that Albert knew his stuff and had some ideas for new products, bang up to date that would sell fast. Albert sketched out some of his ideas for Alec. He was amazed how they were useable and functional but looked amazing and up to date. Designs that no other furniture maker had.

What a talent, Alec thought to himself.

"Well Albert, I just love your ideas, and I would like to offer you the job as a cabinet maker, and I am willing to pay you for any of your designs that we put into production, his does that sound?"

Albert agreed to Alec's proposals, and he was to start the following Monday. He went home feeling elated. Someone had recognised his talent at last. He could not wait to tell Mary Ellen

He rushed down the hall to the Living Room where MaryEllen was laying the table for tea.

He swept her off her feet and swung her round, "be careful you ugly lump! The baby is due in 4 weeks' time, if you carry on like this, it will be born tonight!"

"Aah, Mary Ellen, I have just landed a dream job in woodworking with that modern furniture company down by the Tyne, owned by a cockney geezer called Alec. He wants to create some of my designs, and I will make them. He says he has seen nothing like these in London, and now he can make and market them in the Northeast.

"So Bonny Lass, I will go away to the off-license and get a couple of bottles of beers to celebrate, what do you want?"

"Just an orange juice Albert."

"Keep my dinner warm, pet, back in a moment."

Mary Ellen was dumbfounded. "What is wrong with him!"

What she didn't know, that Albert was not going to tell her the truth, was that Alec was going to write up an agreement to buy his designs outright and pay him the sum of £50 plus for each one depending on size etc., Albert had 20 designs which he reckoned the least he would get was £1,000. "Bloody hell man, who's a clever bugger then?"

Albert had more sketches which needed finishing and would show them to Alec tomorrow.

He whistled all the way to the Off License to get the beers and orange juice and stop at the Chip Shop for 2 Battered Cod and Chips, why not? He could afford this and would keep Mary Ellen sweet. The way I am feeling, it just may be her lucky night, been a while since I gave her one!

The next day Albert went to see Alec with the rest of his designs and to sign the agreement for the sale of his 20 designs.

Alec was an astute businessperson and knew his furniture business well. He had started as an apprentice to his Father in East London as a 15-year-old and learned from the best.

His Father died 15 years ago and left the business to Alec. Alec had the foresight to make designs that were unique, excellent quality and beautiful to look at. He was remarkably successful.

He decided that he would branch out and make a cheaper version of his furniture so that the middle and lower classes could enjoy it. He opened branches in Liverpool and Manchester, targeting his buyers, and within a few years, his name was known by all the furniture buyers in the Midlands.

Alec thought it was time to go further North and decided, after some research, to plump for Newcastle upon Tyne. So, he opened a factory on City Road. He loved the setting up in a new area and he liked the Geordies, so friendly, down to earth, and called a spade a spade.

He was excited about Albert's designs. They were different, very saleable and would bring in a good return. This man had an eye for shape, form, and bringing high-end pieces of furniture affordable to the working class. Albert did not know how good he was.

Alec met Albert at the Reception and gave him a tour of the workshop. There were 10 tradesmen working at their benches and machines. The air was filled with the smell of newly cut wood, sawdust, wood glue and varnish.

Alec took Albert into his office and asked Doris, his secretary, to make them some tea and biscuits.

Doris promptly arrived with the tea tray, and Alec did the pouring. "How do you like yours Albert?"

"Milk and 2 sugars, please."

"Help yourself to biscuits."

Albert looked at the biscuits, chocolate, ginger, and shortbread. At home, they only bought the broken biscuits from Lizzy's corner shop.

Alec had Albert's designs laid out on his desk. "I am excited to put these into production Albert, hugely different and modern, exactly what we need. So, are we agreed that I buy your designs outright? All 20 @ £50 each and I own the copyright to them. You also will start work here in 3 weeks' time to oversee these designs from start to finish, for example, the ordering of materials needed, set up, production and finishing of these designs and marketing.

"You will receive a salary of £30 per week to start plus free meals in our canteen. Our cook Maisie's pies are to die for Albert!

"I have written down the Terms of our Agreement, which you read and sign, and we will get Doris to witness it. All ok with you Albert?" He nodded his head.

"Okay then, we will get Doris in now and I will write you a cheque made out to cash for you to take to the bank."

All signed and completed, Albert left the factory in a dream on his way to the Bank. He felt the cheque on the inside of his jacket and could not believe what had just happened. For once in his life, someone appreciated his work, and he felt elated, a feeling Albert had not experienced before. Humbled!

A Newcastle Lass

Chapter Thirty-Five
In the money

Albert made his way to the Bank on Collingwood Street and cashed his cheque. The teller asked how he would like the notes: £50, £20 or £10? Albert never had to make a decision like that in his life, so he said, "Make it a mixture."

The teller counted out the notes and said, "Would sir like a bag for this?"

Albert said, "Yes please," he had thought that the money would just fit in his pockets.

He folded the Canvas bag and put it inside his coat for safety.

Albert was feeling a little bit guilty at not telling Mary Ellen exactly how much he had been paid. Well, they are my designs and my money, so what if I tell a white lie? Walking home, he had decided to tell her the designs were sold at £ 10 each, earning him a £100 Quid. He will give Mary Ellen £25 to help with the housekeeping. He also stopped off at The Northern Goldsmith's Jewellers and bought a gold ring with a small garnet stone set between 2 tiny pearls. He had asked the assistant in the shop that he wanted a nice ring. But no dearer than £25, this one he liked, and it was only £21.2s.6p. The assistant put it in a ring box and gift-wrapped it. Mary Ellen had never got an engagement ring, so this would make her happy.

When he got home, it was almost 5 o'clock, and he could smell liver and onions cooking. Little Brenda rushed down the hall to meet him, "Did you buy me some sweeties, Daddy?" Brenda just loved getting sweets. He brought out a bag of liquorice all-sorts from his pocket, which she took and ran away to eat them. Typical Brenda, not one for affection or thank you's, just like her old Dad he thought.

Mart Ellen was setting the table for the dinner. "Mary Ellen, stop that for a minute; I have something for you. Come here." Albert said, "I never got you an engagement ring before we were married, so now that I have sold my designs and made a little money, I bought you this… better late than never." Mary Ellen opened the little brown leather box and saw the most beautiful ring she had ever set eyes upon. Albert took it out of the box and put it on her finger.

Mary Ellen was crying. "It is beautiful, thank you, Albert."

"One more surprise, here is £25 to go towards the housekeeping and buy yourself something nice too. We are moving up in the world, pet and this is just the start!"

Mary Ellen kissed him and kept looking at her ring. She forgot all about questioning him. Things were changing, she saw him as the man she fell in love with. He was ready to be a caring Husband and Dad.

Albert was content now. He had money in his pocket, a new job where he was in charge and earning good money. He thought Alec was an honest man and was looking forward to this new challenge to prove to Alec that he knew what he was capable of.

Three weeks passed amazingly fast, and today was the day Albert was starting his new job. He arrived at work just as Alec was opening.

"Morning Albert, my someone's keen, ready to start then? Let us have a mug of tea before anyone else arrives, I will put the kettle on."

After about 15 minutes, the rest of the workforce arrived ready for a new week. Alec had spoken to the workers and explained about Albert and his designs. They were all interested in the drawings and were keen to make this new concept a success. Alex explained that Albert would oversee ordering the materials and the overseeing of the production.

The first few pieces of furniture he had chosen were to test the market. One was a coffee table in polished teak, and the other a matching room divider. The style of these were innovative pieces of furniture new to the industry and to the public.

Albert got to know the workers and thought they were a talented team of blokes. They were all skilled craftsmen, and he knew they would be able to create these designs with no problem.

First, he would need infantry of all types, quantities, and grades of all materials in stock. It took all morning, but this needed to be done.

He asked Doris to put together a list of suppliers and earlier clients.

Albert was in his glory; he just loved the challenge to prove what he was capable of. Plus, the fact that Alec believed he could do the job at hand. At last, someone believed his worth. He would not let Alec down, he had a lot to prove.

The first weeks flew by. Albert was early to work and late to leave. Gathering all the information together on suppliers and past clients, etc. He had a picture in his mind of how he could resource excellent quality timber, varnishes, polishes, waxes at a reasonable price. He worked out the time taken to make a certain piece and cost the job.

He sourced potential new outlets for the modern furniture.

Had the draughtsman make scaled drawings of each of 5 chosen pieces, which were to be a prototype to market. Albert gathered all this information and had a meeting with Alec in his office when the 3 weeks were up.

"Come in, Albert have a seat; I see you have been busy judging by the amount of paperwork you are carrying."

Albert laid out all the information he had gathered and explained in detail to Alec his findings.

Alec listened carefully and kept silent until Albert had finished.

"Well, what do you think, Alec?" asked Albert nervously.

"It all makes perfect sense, Albert. You certainly have been thorough and thought of everything. I am amazed at the amount of researching you have done. You have some refreshing ideas on materials, suppliers, client base etc. I do believe this could work. We need something new that no one else has but is also cost-effective too, and you seem to have covered all these things. Well done lad. We will meet up tomorrow morning and make a start on it, okay? Think you have put in enough hours today time you went home to your wife.

"When is the baby due?"

"Soon," said Albert.

Albert was beaming with happiness when he got home. "Mary Ellen, Alec has agreed to all the suggestions I have made and says we can start to produce soon. How great is that?"

"Oh Albert, I knew you could do it, I am so proud of you!"

After their dinner, they sat by the fire and for once in a long time, Albert fell asleep in his chair. He was exhausted and never happier in his life. Even Mary Ellen did not seem so bad after all. Life is looking up.

Everything was going well for Albert. For once in his life, he felt appreciated for his talent; he would not let Alec down.

He got straight down on the task ahead and relished the thought that he was in charge, and made sure this opportunity he had been given would all come to fruition. A lot of challenging work ahead of him, and he needed to show Alec results fast.

Forward three weeks, Albert had gained orders from new outlets, orders from companies on their books and even some private commissions.

Time to start incorporating some of his other designs.

Well strictly, they belonged to Alec now, as he had bought the rights to them. A meeting with Alex confirmed what Albert had been thinking about: a few more designs going into production. Alec said yes to Albert's plan and to choose himself, which ones would go into the market in the next few weeks. Albert was grinning ear to ear when he went home that night.

As he opened the front door, he heard Mary Ellen's crying in pain.

He rushed through to the kitchen where a neighbour was with her. "Quickly Albert, get the midwife, think your bairn is coming tonight," shouted the neighbour, Mrs. Duggan.

Mary Ellen gave birth to a daughter at 10 to midnight. As she looked at her tiny face, it so reminded her of her mam, Isabella.

"Mam, I miss you so much, but every time I look into her face, I see you there and know you will always be with me. Mam, this is your granddaughter, Irene."

Irene Richardson

Author's Note

I never met my Grandmother Isabella but have always felt a strong connection with her and especially when writing this book, I know her more.

Not long before my Mum, Mary Ellen, passed away, I asked her to tell me a bit more about Isabella, my grandmother, and what did she look like? I had no photo of her.

After a few moments, with tears rolling down her cheeks, she said to me.

"Irene, look in the mirror, and you will see her, and you will know her."

I believe everyone has a guardian angel… mine is Isabella.

Printed in Dunstable, United Kingdom